Citizenship

> This book provides a thoughtful approach to citizenship grounded in both classical and contemporary political science, making it a sound foundation for students becoming familiar with literature on citizenship.
>
> —Arthur Sementelli, *Florida Atlantic University, USA*

This groundbreaking book covers the full spectrum of literature on citizenship theory, including the state and structure of identity, the individual and the public, and the enduring issues of civic engagement and collective discourse. It examines some of the complex challenges faced by citizens and policy makers and explores the existing procedural and institutional mechanisms that undermine democratic political accountability as well as its legitimation.

From classical conceptions of citizenship in the early Greco-Roman eras to contemporary critical social theory and postmodernist contentions, author Kalu N. Kalu covers complex issues including rights and obligation, the doctrine of state sovereignty and authority, equality, the principle of majority rule, citizen participation in governance, public versus self-interest, ideas of justice, immigration and cultural identity, global citizenship, and the evolution of hybrid communities that challenge traditional notions of state-citizenship identity. With meticulous detail and powerful analysis, this book illuminates the intellectual richness of citizenship literature on the one hand while demonstrating the ongoing challenges in both conceptualization and practice on the other.

Kalu N. Kalu is Distinguished Research Professor of Political Science & National Security Policy at Auburn University Montgomery, USA and Docent Professor at the University of Tampere, Finland.

Citizenship

Identity, Institutions and the Postmodern Challenge

Kalu N. Kalu

Routledge
Taylor & Francis Group
NEW YORK AND LONDON

First published 2017
by Routledge
711 Third Avenue, New York, NY 10017

and by Routledge
2 Park Square, Milton Park, Abingdon, Oxon OX14 4RN

Routledge is an imprint of the Taylor & Francis Group, an informa business

Library of Congress Cataloging in Publication Data

Names: Kalu, Kalu Ndukwe, author.
Title: Citizenship: identity, institutions, and the postmodern challenge / by Kalu N. Kalu.
Description: New York, NY: Routledge, 2016. | Includes bibliographical references and index.
Identifiers: LCCN 2016004517 | ISBN 9781482223248 (cloth: alk. paper) |
ISBN 9781315538143 (ebook)
Subjects: LCSH: Citizenship.
Classification: LCC JF801 .K35 2016 | DDC 323.6—dc23
LC record available at http://lccn.loc.gov/2016004517

ISBN: 978-1-4822-2324-8 (hbk)
ISBN: 978-1-315-53814-3 (ebk)

Typeset in Times New Roman
by codeMantra

For
Reneé Elizabeth Aluba N. Kalu
Sebastian Ulysses Ikechukwu N. Kalu
Joy Kalu
Glory Kalu

Contents

Contents

List of Figures and Tables

Figures

Tables

Preface

The preparation for this book took on increasingly greater importance for me, particularly in light of current events around the world, most of which will certainly impact on our traditional notions of citizenship, identity and the concept of the sovereign state. It is in this context that I view this book as timely both in regards to the manifold issues addressed and also as a way of illuminating the central arguments concerning citizenship and the various epistemological emphasis that seems to surround contemporary debate on the subject matter. This work also raises an important issue about the effectiveness of citizen participation in governance and how it has been used to legitimize policies that may, in fact, be detrimental to citizens' interests. It also draws upon the issue of information asymmetry, trust, the role of social structure and stratification in public discourse and political power such that in the process of citizen-agency exchange all parties to the engagement generally operate from different sets of priorities, obligations, and value judgments that may be both incommensurable and irreconcilable.

I draw from an extensive literature on different philosophical traditions, from classical antiquity in the Greek and Roman traditions to the more contemporary canons in the traditions of neo-republican citizenship, communitarian citizenship, multicultural, and differentiated citizenship. One often comes out with a sense that citizenship is a construct that is continuously contested, but this is a theoretical mistake that still begs the question, as well as desires answers. In what ways and on what basis is citizenship being contested even while those who 'contest' it are actually experiencing as well as benefiting from its advantages? The point is that the construct of citizenship exists, and what should be contested is not its existence, but the differential meanings which we make of it. The profound irony in all these is that if and when we have competing understandings of the same phenomenon, there can be only two possible explanations. Either no one understands what the phenomenon is, or we have chosen to give it our own definitions by virtue of our own independent experiences.

To me, acceding to each of the above positions is fair enough, but what should not be lost is the fact that citizenship has traditionally been construed as a form of right in lieu of the state. If we accept this premise as a common denominator, then other conceptual differences matter very little since, after all, they all share the same elan or reality at the core. While the postmodern contention denies the existence of the kind of shared reality that citizenship enables, it also argues that we cannot surmise all issues of this world in one over-arching grand narrative. Therefore people can, in fact, construct their own realities of what is 'out there' by virtue of their own individual experiences. But even if this account is accepted as hypothetical truth, still such individual experiences are validated within the context of a state and the privileges offered by the institutions and laws that pertain to it.

By subjecting this evident reality to endless deconstructive analysis we, more often than not, find ourselves caught up, in Kierkegaardian terms, between the unconditioned character of the existential resolve as against the conditioned nature of the objectified sensory world; between an uncontrolled imagination and the epistemological relativism through which we attempt to make sense of our daily experiences. But as Hannah Arendt points out, in the realm of ideas, there are only originality and depth, no absolutes; hence, ideas can only acquire aura or permanency depending upon their inherent power of illumination which, invariably, endures independently of time and history. It therefore becomes incumbent on us to rise above our conceptual narratives to engage in what really matters—the art and practice of citizenship.

Kalu N. Kalu
Auburn University Montgomery

About the Author

Kalu N. Kalu is Distinguished Research Professor of Political Science & National Security Policy at Auburn University Montgomery, Docent Professor at the University of Tampere, Finland and a Fulbright Scholar. He has been a Research Affiliate at The Whitney and Betty Macmillan Center for International and Area Studies, Yale University, and a Visiting Senior Research Fellow at the Nigerian Institute of International Affairs. He is also a recipient of two certificates in Joint Strategic Leadership and National Security Decision Making from the United States Air War College (2010–2011). Professor Kalu is widely published with articles in leading peer-reviewed journals and has a combined production of over 60 scholarly works cumulatively in terms of publications in journals, books, edited volumes and in national and international conference presentations.

His research emphasis is in the areas of comparative institutions and development, organization theory and organizational change, citizenship and administrative theory, technology-leadership-culture interface, complex adaptive systems, national security and intelligence policy, and health care politics and policies. He has been invited to and participated in several international learned conferences in various countries around the world including Canada, Germany, Italy, Norway, Finland, Switzerland, Saudi Arabia, United Arab Emirates, China, Singapore and India. He has served as a member of the National Council of the American Society for Public Administration and on the Editorial Board of *Public Administration Review*, the premier journal in the field. He is the author of *State Power, Autarchy, and Political Conquest in Nigerian Federalism* (*Rowman & Littlefield Publishers, 2008*); and *Citizenship: A Reality Far from Ideal* (co-edited with Nada Kakabadse and Andrew Kakabadse, 2009).

1 Epistemological Foundations of Citizenship Theory

The concept of citizenship has been going through a modern-day transformation for the past 40 years, and this, rather unfortunately, seems to have added to the continuing epistemological confusion about what the concept stands for and how we go about validating it. The further we explore, the deeper we delve into a long process of inquiry and discovery. What in the end is citizenship? Is it a matter of individual or collective happiness in the *polis* or of equality of rights and opportunity for all? How do we distribute collective rights and opportunities in such a way that no one feels disenfranchised as long as he or she maintains the entitlement to citizenship? The foregoing calls into question the twin issues of justice and fairness, because to be availed of the benefits of citizenship, the distributive mechanism associated with equal opportunity and access to public goods and services must be considered fair and just. In this context, citizenship offers a placeholder for the ideal of justice for all, but whose definition of justice?

As a construct, citizenship is like a fulcrum, holding together the spokes on a bicycle wheel as they each branch outwards, none too far removed from the other spokes so that, collectively, they all provide the support needed to keep the wheel revolving and in motion. For every energy and effort that is directed toward turning the wheel and directing it to its purpose—keeping it in motion—a stark reality emerges, and that is: There is an intrinsic logic between effort and motion that must be consistently sustained in order to maintain the activity. In its socio-political context, citizenship is a principle of constitutional reconstruction, in the sense that while citizens play an active role in it, the Constitution on the other hand seeks to foster citizenship among the people (van Gunsteren, 1998, p. 7). When the laws of a republic are made by the will of the people, and when they obey the principles and regulations that inform that law, they end up granting authority to the individuals who are charged with their implementation. So the citizens of a republic have a dual responsibility: They rule directly by consenting to the laws, but they also obey fellow citizens in their ruling authority as officeholders (van Gunsteren, 1998, p. 7). Both activities provide a nourishing environment for the growth and vitality of the republic as well as citizenship.

Competing Postulates in Contemporary Discourse: Whither Equality?

The contemporary conceptualization in citizenship theory suggests different strands that are oftentimes conflated with each other: "*citizenship-as-legal-status*, that is, as full membership in a particular political community; *citizenship-as-desirable-activity*, where the extent and quality of one's citizenship is a function of one's participation in that community" (Kymlicka and Norman, 1994, p. 353); and *citizenship-as-obligation*, where citizenship is considered as a function of having paid one's dues by virtue of being a citizen. But by contrasting *citizenship-as-activity* with an alternate conception of *citizenship-as-status*, we prematurely limit the argument as to whether citizenship can be considered a matter of rights grounded in statehood or conferred by law.

As one of the early pioneers in citizenship theory, T.H. Marshall (1965, p. 117) cautioned that the preservation of economic inequalities has been made more difficult by the enrichment of the status of citizenship. "Instead of accepting citizenship as a political and social status, modern conservatives have sought to reassert the role of the market (wealth and wealth creation) and have rejected the idea that citizenship confers a status independent of economic standing" (Kymlicka and Norman, 1994, p. 357). At the heart of Marshall's account of citizenship "lies the contradiction between the formal political equality of the franchise and the persistence of extensive social and economic inequality, ultimately rooted in the character of the capitalist market place and the existence of private property" (Turner, 1990, p. 191). Hence "through education in its relations with occupational structure, citizenship operates as an instrument of social stratification" (Marshall, 1965, p. 110). Marshall therefore sees citizenship as a shared identity that integrates previously excluded groups (especially in British society) and provides a source of national unity. He is particularly concerned with integrating the working classes, whose lack of education and economic resources excludes them from the 'common culture'—that should have been a 'common possession and heritage.'

In most postwar political theory, "the fundamental normative concepts were democracy (for evaluating procedures) and justice (for evaluating outcomes). Citizenship was usually seen as a derivative of democracy and justice—that is, a citizen is someone who has democratic rights and claims of justice" (Kymlicka and Norman, 1994, p. 369). For Marshall, the fullest expression of citizenship requires a liberal democratic welfare state that can guarantee basic civil, political and social rights. "Where any of these rights is withheld or violated, people will be marginalized and unable to participate" (Marshall, 1965, p. 78). This is often called "passive" or "private" citizenship "because of its emphasis on passive entitlements and the absence of any obligation to participate in public life" (Kymlicka and Norman, 1994, p. 354). Hence, "the challenge of contemporary advocates of citizenship theory is how to reconcile the passive acceptance of citizenship rights with the active exercise of citizenship responsibilities and virtues, including economic self-reliance, political participation, and even civility" (Kymlicka and Norman, 1994, p. 355).

In further exploring the active-passive trajectory of citizenship theory, I draw from a modified view of Richard Flathman's (1981) citizenship typology. In this regard, "high citizenship" suggests that citizens are free, equal and engaged with one another in pursuing matters of high and distinctive human import. As a distinctly human activity, citizenship thus becomes the most important feature of political society. Under conditions of "low citizenship," the ideal of "high citizenship" is unachievable and hence would be irrelevant to political life and practice in the modern state. Nonetheless, the continuous, intense, morally uplifting interactions, which the ideal presumes, can be obtained, if at all, only among sub-groups within the large, complex and impersonal societies of the modern world. Hence, as some argue, "citizenship is unlikely to be the primary identity or the consuming passion of men and women living in complex and highly differentiated societies, where politics competes for time and attention with class, ethnicity, religion, and family, and where these latter four do not draw people together but rather separate and divide them" (Walzer, 1989, p.218). The simple fact is that where and "when the scale of political organization changes, unity and trust collapse and a different understanding of citizenship may be required" (Walzer, 1989, p.214).

This brings us back to the issue of political participation as a central part of the ideal of civic republicanism. We know that Machiavelli's *Discourses on Livy* stands as a case study in civic Republican politics. To the extent that it encourages political participation (without the exclusionary clauses), it represents a wholesome expression of positive liberalism. Civic republicanism sees political participation as instrumental in bringing about political liberty; hence, to the extent that it is a good indication of virtue, people can discover themselves through participation in politics. The unanswered question remains, however, especially from the perspective of cultural pluralists who advocate a kind of differentiated citizenship that caters to the unique realities and experiences of each group. It therefore still begs the question: How can I discover myself through political participation when the institutional context for participation is not structured to reflect what I consider to be the isolated circumstance of my own existence?

The Exercise of Private and Public Rights

The rights and privileges acquired as an entitlement of citizenship serve two complementary purposes: that of the individual in the isolation of his or her private life and that of the individual in his or her inclusiveness as part of the political community to which he or she belongs. But for the purpose of citizenship, the exercise of rights in one or the other cannot be mutually exclusive except in situations where the exercise of a specific right must of necessity come into conflict with other competing rights claims in the larger community. This is reinforced by the fact that the calculation of rights and the degree to which they complement or diverge from similar rights claims of others is a matter of qualitative judgment that can, oftentimes, be quite subjective. Because very few rights claims, particularly those related to issues of justice and fairness, are amenable to concrete analysis or discrete evidence, we are nonetheless forced to rely on mundane and everyday practices and cultural narratives to make determinations about the validity and circumstances in which specific rights will or will not prevail.

Hence, how we construct a theory of citizenship is therefore a matter of how we adjudicate rights claims in the private and public space and the consistency that is evident in the execution of their substantive and procedural requirements. The liberal-individualist approach sees rights as a matter of individual prerogative in which choice is defined by citizens' calculations of their own rights within the limits of their respect for the rights of others. However, the problem remains as to how to know where and when the limits of individual choice have been reached and how individuals acting in their own rational self-interest can be relied upon to make the right decisions and choices all of the time. The alternative communitarian argument holds that being a citizen involves belonging to a historically developed community; therefore, whatever the individual has is derived and circumscribed by the customs, tradition and practices of the community (van Gunsteren, 1998, p. 19). While this may seem logical, it does not help to explain the character of the existing communal life or the processes that shape collective deliberations and cultural development within it. It does not fully explain the dynamics by which individual moral agency transcends the collective agency necessary for individual and community well-being.

But as is the case in many liberal democracies, it is very difficult to achieve universal consensus on critical communal issues. Even where agreements on central issues are achieved by way of the principle of majority rule, minorities who may have superior and evidence-based disagreements on the merits of the customs, traditions and practices of the community are still circumscribed to live under conditions they disagree with. While acceptance of communitarian values can help to facilitate collective action in addressing community problems, agreement on the basis of and justification for those values is also necessary. Because of this, communitarians need to develop a more comprehensive framework for resolving disagreements within community-based value structures, as well as individual differences when issues of private and public good come into conflict.

In line with the Aristotelian thesis of political participation in the interest of the *polis* as a form of active citizenship, the republican theory of citizenship places the public community (the state or *polis*) at the center of political life. While recognizing individuality, "individuals can mark their place in history by serving the public community, and through this, they can find fulfillment and happiness" (van Gunsteren, 1998, p. 21). In a similar vein, Bryan Turner (1990, p. 193) argues that a theory of citizenship must also produce a theory of the state. He points out that the state provides the principal element in the maintenance and development of social rights, as it is the political instrument through which political movements seek to redress their circumstances through the legitimization of their claims against society.

While the idea of claims implies an expression of rights, the issue that Aristotle's republicanism raises is how these rights become legitimate or authentic, that is, granted some fundamental entitlements backed by law. In an Aristotelian world, the criteria for guaranteeing citizenship rights include wealth, property and participation. The state exists solely for noble actions: "Those who do noble deeds are contributing to the quality of political association, and those who contribute most are entitled to a larger share than those who, though they may be equal or even superior in birth and family, but are inferior in noble deeds and so in the essential goodness they bring to the *polis*/community" (Aristotle, 1962, p. 121). Hence "citizenship as a *social value* seeks to motivate individuals toward civic virtue, patriotism, and volunteerism" (Halisi, 1998, p. 340).

Of Differentiated and Multicultural Citizenship and Their Ends

Some of the more central arguments in citizenship theory revolve around the four basic constructs of equality, obligation, rights and entitlements. Because the state and its institutions serve as the primary anchor upon which each of these could be realized, the content and form of each would essentially be shaped according to the interests of the state. Hence "citizenship rights reflect the societies in which they are created" (Janoski and Gran, 2002, p. 25). On the premise that nature endows, but endows differently, the temporal world in which we live is a world of differences with regard to each individual life's burden as well as its benefits. While it is one thing to preach equality as a universal norm, it is another to attempt to achieve a common denominator to which everyone would agree as a reflection of equality both in treatment and in access. So when we speak of equality-in-practice, we are actually talking about relative equality as opposed to absolute equality.

Both Plato and Aristotle recognize that the idea of equality is untenable and that nature itself did not seek to create all human beings as equals: not necessarily with respect to their humanness but to the fact that nature grants each and every person different gifts or talents ranging from intuition, physique, oratory, gamesmanship, mathematics, music and other qualities too numerous to mention. Differences and inequalities occur as a result of the fact that nature accords each and every individual with different attributes. A good society therefore would be one that recognizes and, in fact, applies these inequalities in the arrangement of the social structure and in the allocation of individual functions and rewards in society.

Plato's ideal state requires the division of society into three, comprising the rulers (who possess the natural or God-given qualities of intuition and virtue and hence should become the rulers and decision makers for the *polis*); the guardians (who have been gifted with strength and physique and hence should be assigned to become soldiers for the defense of the state); and the laborers (who have neither the intelligence of the rulers nor the strength of the guardians and are therefore assigned to roles that mainly enable them to facilitate the nobler activities of the rulers and the guardians). On his own account, Aristotle divides society into two broad themes of the wealthy and the poor: the wealthy being those who have money and property and are able to pay taxes for the maintenance of the state and hence should be considered true citizens and would be desiring of holding public office. However, in an Aristotelian state, the poor and the super-annuated should not be considered citizens because in their own special circumstances they are less likely or able to contribute to the maintenance and defense of the state. This form of social stratification has historically shaped how we conceive of citizenship as membership, community, entitlement or right and obligation even in contemporary society.

The sociologist Karl Marx classified social organization and work into the two classes of the bourgeoisie (owners of the factors of production) and the proletarians (the workers whose exploitation helps to create the surplus value critical to capitalist wealth accumulation). While both classes play differentiated roles in society, they also share differentiated benefits: the former enormous wealth, profits and power and the latter 'wretchedness' and subsistence living. In all societies, there are categories of differences such as rich and poor, male and female, white-collar and blue-collar workers, upper-income and lower-income, young and old, liberal and conservative, white, black or brown, and several others.

However, while each may share a similar and common understanding on such normative issues as justice, equality, fairness and due process, and to the extent that each may experience different levels of effect or experience regarding the social application of these norms and values, citizenship rights may seek to recognize the different circumstances and experiences of each of the categories within the more encompassing rights and privileges of all. The state's attempt to construct a *civic public* premised on equality of treatment and access regarding these normative values can thus be broadened to accommodate these differences. Hence the republican quest for the common good is capable of accommodating the interests of those who stand in social locations different from that of the more privileged who are in a better position to determine the nature and character of the common good.

Differentiated Citizenship

In contemporary citizenship studies, one of the most influential theorists of what is known as "cultural pluralism" (differentiated citizenship) is Iris Marion Young. According to Young (1989), the attempt to create a universal conception of citizenship, which transcends group differences, is fundamentally unjust because it oppresses historically excluded groups. Hence, culturally excluded groups often have distinctive needs that can be met only through group-differentiated policies. The general premise is that genuine equality requires us to affirm rather than ignore group differences. The view of citizenship as generality presupposes that "whatever the social or group differences among citizens, whatever their inequalities of wealth, status, and power in the everyday activities of civil society, citizenship gives everyone the same status as peers in the political public" (Young, 1998, p. 263). However, she criticizes this point, arguing instead that defining citizenship as generality avoids and obscures the requirement that all experiences, needs and perspectives on social events have a voice and should be respected. She states that, "even though all citizens have the right to participate in the decision-making process, the experience and perspectives of some groups tend to be silenced for many reasons" (Young, 1998, p. 271).

"Group differences involve not only different needs, interests, and goals, but also different social locations and experiences from which social facts and policies are understood" (Young, 1998, p. 277); hence, no one can claim to speak for the public interest. The "only ground for a claim that a policy or decision is just is that it has been arrived at by a public that has truly promoted free expression of all needs and points of view; group representation is the best means to promote just outcomes to democratic decision-making processes" (Young, 1998, p. 276). The kind of differentiated citizenship that she professes is one that offers considerations, benefits and opportunities based on the unique realities and circumstances of social groups.

While this view poses the challenge of how we go about creating a human community with a unified sense of purpose and mutual interest, it suggests that citizenship as a group construct is relative. If we reduce it to a moral imperative, then it becomes an entitlement that can be awarded on the basis of our differences rather than our commonalities. In this regard, citizenship would be yet another force for disunity, rather than a way of cultivating unity in the face of increasing social diversity (Kymlicka, 1995a, p. 175). "The homogeneity required for collective deliberation on the common good no longer exists and could only be reintroduced at the drastic cost of a gross simplification and curtailment of human creativity and interaction" (Bellamy and Schecter, 1993, p. 162). Pluralist democracies recognize group differences, but they do not see them as mutually exclusive categories; rather they structure the process of public deliberation in such a way that all perspectives are part of the discussion, and choices are made based on majority rule. "For support and comfort and a sense of belonging, men and women, invariably, look to their groups; but for freedom and mobility, they look to the state" (Walzer, 1995, p. 148). Hence, democratic pluralism helps to "bring group members into the political arena where they are likely to discover common interests" (Walzer, 1995, p. 148).

Multicultural Citizenship

An extended discussion on differentiated citizenship includes a focus on group rights as an additional reinforcement of individual rights. Will Kymlicka's multicultural citizenship argues that the adoption of group-specific poly-ethnic representation or self-government within the broader national policy would encourage inclusion and integration. He points out that in "most countries where groups have been excluded from full political participation it was not because of their socioeconomic status, but rather because of their socio-cultural identity—their *difference*" (Kymlicka, 1998, p. 173); and given this dynamic, "imposing citizenship on minorities that view themselves as distinct nations or peoples would likely increase conflict in a multination state" (Kymlicka, 1998, p. 177). To the extent that Kymlicka's argument focuses on the primary importance of individual autonomy expressed and protected within the context of the all-encompassing cultural rights of groups, it seeks to "guarantee a cultural environment within which the individual is able to exercise the capacity to make meaningful choices" (Kukathas, 1995b, p. 241). By granting specific rights and autonomy to cultural groups, we are able to mitigate the structural impediments of majority-minority status on community decision making as well as in the representativeness of the choices that result from it.

The multicultural thesis has been challenged by others who argue that "citizenship cannot perform its vital integrative function if it is differentiated; it ceases to be a device to cultivate a sense of community and a common sense of purpose" (Heater, 1990, p. 295). While the argument may seem to cut both ways, the point is that if treated well and in an inclusive manner, differentiated groups could possibly develop the integrative norms critical to the building of collective membership. But because multiculturalism seeks the acknowledgment and treatment of distinct social categories differently, groups are more likely to choose to be viewed differently as long as the rights and benefits of being viewed as such by the state outweighs the disadvantages of the more generic alternative of being viewed as the same as everyone else. And "this may encourage group leaders to devote their political energy to establishing a perception of disadvantage; rather than working to overcome it in order to secure their claim to group rights" (Kymlicka and Norman, 1994, p. 372).

When citizenship and membership of a community is adjudicated on the basis of comparative advantage or as a matter of choice between group and national identity, then its role as an integrative phenomenon is lost or, at best, becomes contingent. This contingency suggests that community in the sense that communitarians hold it is simply a *constructed public*, because it provides a public space for membership and collective discourse. What it will become or how well it will advance the purpose of communal flourishing can only be determined by the characteristics of the membership and the qualities of habit (virtue) and aspirations (identity and motive) they bring to it. In this regard, the purpose and importance of the community represents a public project, while generally obvious in the minds of the members, a project whose true realization is contingent on yet far removed from the practical realities of the moment. The idea of contingency is important because the framework upon which communities are founded is very fluid and, in most cases, unpredictable. In the same way that communities can be formed and purposefully organized, they can also be dissolved or disbanded. Its sustainability depends on the mutuality of interests and the scope of distributive benefits and opportunities it offers as a means of satisfying each member's individual interests.

The Good Citizen and Postmodern Interpretivism

Two primary qualifications have remained ubiquitous in most discussions of citizenship: the *good* and the *bad* citizen. A proper understanding of why the two qualifiers have become relevant necessitates us to also understand the concept of the good, particularly since anything that is not comparatively *good* would most likely be *bad.* An act or behavior is considered *good* if it serves a specific aim sought by a person or a purpose for which the *goodness* of an objective is sought as a matter of satisfying some individual need or political and social convention. It is also necessary to qualify the point that a resultant *good* may be attributed to the effort and resources put into seeking a particular good, or it may be due to the valence or value attached to an expected *good* (outcome) by those who stand to benefit from it.

For Aristotle (1985, p. 406), results are good insofar as someone aiming at the results has reason to aim at them. In this case, a good becomes conditioned on achieving the objective that is aimed at. A good can also be attributed to a person, animal, machine, object, food, house, automobile or anything that satisfactorily serves the purpose for which it was meant or that was expected. An illustrative example is provided in Aristotle's *Nicomachean Ethics* (1985, p. 406), in which he points out that "a good horse is a good specimen of horses—but its goodness is determined by what horses characteristically do and can be expected to do, that is the *function* of horses. Similarly, a good person is one who does well what persons can be expected to do and also has virtue appropriate to persons." The type of virtue that Aristotle advocates is one that is teleologically connected to the goodness of the community.

Although the act of goodness may originate from the fact that virtue is able to direct the rational acts of man toward a specific *telos* that is good, a "person is not an artifact or an organ, and his goodness (virtue) is not to be measured by his use, but by his own intrinsic good—his *happiness*" (Aristotle, 1985, p. 407). Therefore, to seek goodness is not an end in itself, but it is a means for achieving that objective that serves a specific aim that represents *goodness*. Oftentimes goodness is a sentiment that expresses a sense of approval or the satisfaction that an act or process has resulted in something that is valuable—the *goodness* as reflected in such things as having peace of mind, a feeling of comfort or happiness. These are not expressions of goodness in and of themselves, since they only provide the pathways for securing the good. When a person has a feeling of comfort, it means that he does not experience pain; in the same way, when he feels a sense of happiness and the inner serenity that goes with it, he does not have anger. But it is by avoiding anger that the person can be said to be happy. The idea of goodness, in this regard, is achieved through the negative feedback of avoiding anger. Because an individual can only be happy by avoiding the more deleterious alternative of being angry, the essence of *goodness* is reflected in the negation of anger but not in the attainment of happiness *per se*.

Although Aristotle sees happiness as self-sufficient and as an end in itself, he also sees it as virtuous action (Aristotle, 1985, p. 282). According to him, "the happy life seems to be a life expressing virtue, which is a life involving serious actions, and not consisting in amusement; happiness, therefore, is found not in these past-times, but in the activities expressing virtue" (Aristotle, 1985, p. 283). The problem with the Aristotelian thesis is that if the 'expression of virtue involves a series of actions,' these actions must of necessity lead to some other end or value—and one of these other values could be the achievement of *happiness*. He sees this as the type of happiness that leads to *eudaimonia* (an end in itself)—the state of being well and doing well at being well. Because "the virtues are precisely those qualities that will enable an individual to achieve *eudaimonia*, the lack of which will frustrate his movement toward that *telos*" (Kalu, 2003a, p. 421), happiness cannot be its own end. Rather it should be seen as a *contingent* good that often finds expression as a result of an act of goodness or as a state of mind characterized as good (in this case *eudaimonia*). The early *Stoic* Diogenes Laertius educates us that "things are preferred for their own sake because they accord with nature; not for their own sake, but for the sake of something else, because they secure not a few utilities" (Saunders, 1966, p. 119).

Nonetheless, the contemporary dichotomy we apply in consideration of good and bad citizens presents its own problems. In the American context, for example, being a good citizen has to do with a person's role in the political process through active participation, autonomy, independent self-reflection and engagement on critical issues of the democratic discourse and acceptance of state authority and the legitimacy of its laws, as well as embracing the regime's norms and constitutional values that sustain the republic. As idealistic as this may seem, one ought to question to what extent does it resonate within the average American citizen. One ought to ask this most particularly at a time when there has been declining voter turnout in general elections, absence of integrating social capital as Americans turn away from traditional civic obligations and neighborhood associations and an increasing level of partisan dealignment that has seen a dramatic rise in the category of Independents, despite the fact that they have little or no chance of having their own candidate win a national election. As individuals become increasingly frustrated at the inability of government to deal with pressing issues of state and governance, they disengage from the public space as passive participants in the political process.

Others like James Bryce (1993) have argued that among the hindrances to good citizenship are indolence, private self-interest and partisanship. Should we therefore consider an increasing number of Americans as *bad* citizens? I have always maintained that the dichotomy between good and bad citizenship is a misnomer because as a matter of right, further qualifications of merit are unnecessary to justify any and all entitlements to the benefits associated with the status (Kalu, 2003a, p. 425). In a similar vein, Kymlicka and Norman (1994, p. 353) caution that "we should expect a theory of the good citizen to be relatively independent of the legal question of what it is to be a citizen, just as a theory of the good person is distinct from the metaphysical (or legal) question of what it is to be a person."

Furthermore, the concept of the good and bad citizen cannot be construed as a permanent, resilient and unchangeable quality. In the same way that attitudes, circumstances and behaviors can change, a person can be a good citizen most of the time but also a bad citizen at some time, depending on where and under what circumstances he finds himself. The idea of a good or bad citizen is a behavioral characterization that has nothing to do with a person's citizenship status but has to do with what a person does or does not do. To be more practical in this illustration, let us therefore consider a situation where someone committed a serious crime and was sent to jail, where he served his sentence with great remorse for having run afoul of the law. Certainly, we would consider such a person to be a bad citizen. But then he gets out of prison, sobers himself up, gets a great job, avoids traffic violations, pays his taxes, and finds religion along the way. Would we still consider him a *bad* citizen, or is he now a *good* citizen?

Even for some existentialists and postmodernists, the good citizen could be that rebellious self who is able to muster the courage to challenge authority and who seeks to define by and for him- or herself that which embodies his or her own existence. By affirming the self in the lonely isolation of one's individuality, he also affirms it for all, since in essence we all share a common quality—our collective humanity. A classical corollary would be Socrates in the *Phaedo* (See *Great Dialogues of Plato*) when, upon having taken the poison, he called out to Criton: '*We owe a cock to Asclepios; pay it without fail*,' and the other willingly consented. In Greek mythology, sacrificing a cock is meant to be a thank-offering to the god of healing, and by this request, Socrates affirms for all of the continuity of life even after death. It was a sign of the recognition of institutional rules and mores, like paying off one's debt, and atonement for any past misdeeds, but it was also a request for an easy transition from the temporal world to that beyond.

It was, on the one hand, "an attempt to save the *polis* through direct action on the part of individual citizens, in obedience to the command of the gods" (Voegelin, 1957, p. 139). On the other it was an affirmation of the universal belief that obedience to the laws was an act of civic virtue; hence, taking and dying from the poison was a noble deed because death is the opposite of as well as the cure for life. The Roman poet Lucretius (99–55 BC) also reminds us in *De Rerum Natura,* "As for all those torments that are said to take place in the depths of Hell, they are actually present here and now, in our lives" (Saunders, 1966, p. 37). For Socrates, this would be the ultimate vindication of his refusal to heed the consistent pleas from Crito to wait till sunset to take the potion. He felt that his departure from this life to that beyond would free him from all of the troubles of the mortal world; hence his action was a defense of justice, not its repudiation. It was a mark of the *practice* of good citizenship by virtue of *action* in obedience to the law.

Environments of Citizenship

It has remained most evident that the ideal of citizenship cannot be conceived in isolation from the Other, in terms of a common placeholder or context upon which we can experience its significance. It is always seen as *citizenship-in-lieu-of* some other thing, be that the state, activity, achievement, honor, service or sacrifice. Since these "other things" are ontologically associated with citizenship both as a construct and in the way individuals attach meaning to it, it is, therefore, important to isolate the broad categories within which citizenship can find expression as well as legitimacy in both theory and practice. In this regard, I propose four general categories of environments of citizenship: political, individual, social and professional. The perspective developed here draws from the role of citizenship as an institutional status as well as a multidimensional construct feeding on multiple sources of influence for its own validation.

The Political Environment

The political environment of citizenship is grounded in its association to an autonomous state with defined geo-political boundaries and the sovereign authority to make judgments regarding matters of law, rights, justice, entitlements, sanctions and punishments. It is of less consequence whether the state is characterized by a Hobbesian state of absolute rule, a Platonian social stratification, Darwin's survival of the fittest or even in a special case of Orwellian rule; what matters most is the nature of collective agreement (social contract) embodied in the constitutional principles that drive state action. Even though the Constitution may provide specific rights to citizens, it is important to note that within the political environment the expression of rights (excepting in situations of willful or negligent violation) always passes a litmus test of conformity to acceptable political and social conventions and avoids potential conflict in multiple expressions of similarly situated rights claims. The state, through its laws and regulations, circumscribes the scope of free expression of citizenship both as status and as a right conditioned on specific claims. However, in most authoritarian states where fidelity to the tenets of the Constitution may matter less, the functions of the state and its devices are still subject to the discretionary whims of those who shape or are in control of the conditions for exercising political authority.

The international environment and the characteristics of a state's bilateral and multilateral relations with other states in the international community are also part of the political environment of citizenship. From the perspective of realism, as each state seeks to project its own national interests and those of its citizens onto the rest of the international system, it is the projection of power that explains why and how states relate to each other. On the other hand, liberal institutionalists argue that state cooperation through multilateral organizations and economic interdependence would create conditions for peaceful mutual coexistence as each state seeks to preserve and protect gains already achieved through cooperative arrangements on global issues. When states act in the international system, they mostly act in the interest of themselves and their citizens; whether this is done under the rubric of genuine national interest, political expediency or simple hubris is of little importance.

Citizenship is also very much impacted by existing laws and regulations, social conventions, norms and civic engagements such as charity and philanthropy, as well as events and crises in other parts of the international community.

It is an expression of genuine citizenship for individuals to develop the habit of paying their taxes, driving on the correct side of the road, obeying traffic conventions, serving on juries, resisting the urge to litter, waiting their turn in a queue and not drinking while driving. Obedience to the law, donating to charities and doing all you can to make life better for others without the expectation of reward is also being a good citizen. The ability to vote in elections, run for political office, join political parties and interest groups of one's choosing and engage in interest articulation, protest movements, plebiscites and referendums are all activities, though integrally tied to citizenship, that must be equally adjudicated within the existing confines of the state and the political environment.

The political environment also subsumes an economic system that provides opportunity for citizens to have income-earning jobs, develop specific skills in the sciences, arts, literature and technology and fulfill their own individual aspirations within the scope of enabling conditions provided by the state. Independently, citizenship and the state offer partial explanations, but what we conceive as citizenship is nothing but an objectification of the relational properties that emerge as a result of the functional inseparability between state and citizen. The construction of citizenship identity is therefore directed toward infusing meaning into the relationships between the two and how they, now commonly conceived, address critical issues of the human condition.

To the extent that "norms and citizenship are understood as a thing that we build in the process of constructing our identity" (Bendek, 2002, p. 191), we seek an institutional foundation upon which these norms and values could be legitimized and sustained. This reciprocal validation can also draw upon Hannah Arendt's (1958, p. 9) aphorism that "whatever touches or enters into a sustained relationship with human life immediately assumes the character of a condition of human existence; and in this sense, men are conditioned beings because everything they come in contact with turns immediately into a condition of their existence." The state exists and is, more often than not, a reflection of its citizens and vice versa.

The Individual Environment

The individual environment embodies but is not limited to the scope of individual autonomy and judgment, the conditions for the expression of rights and obligations, the responsibilities of and obedience to the founding values of the state and the social and political conventions that are customarily accepted and practiced. As Herman van Gunsteren (1988, p. 732) points out, autonomy in this regard is not construed in the sense of acting alone, nor is judgment the same as stating one's subjective and arbitrary opinion. Rather, autonomy and judgment imply acting, doing and bringing something about in conjunction with others in the political community in such a way that one remains capable of both ruling and being ruled. While the exercise of individual autonomy and judgment is not something we can sustain on our own, these nonetheless help to reinforce an "identity that is partly defined in conversation with others or through the common understanding which underlies the practices of our society" (Taylor, 1992, p. 49).

Therefore, as a free and autonomous individual who affirms himself as such, I also have an obligation to complete, restore or sustain the society within which this identity is possible (Taylor, 1992, p. 49). "Freedom thus requires dependence upon the law so that citizens may be independent of the arbitrary will of others" (Dagger, 2002, p. 147); members of the public must also understand the responsibility "to overcome their personal inclinations and set aside their private interests when necessary to do what is best for the public as a whole" (Dagger, 2002, p. 147). Hence, "nothing is enjoined upon the individual beyond a respect for the autonomy of others and the minimal civic duties of keeping the state in being—voting, paying taxes, or serving in the military" (Oldfield, 1998, p. 77).

The individual environment also comprises the *inner* and *expressed* selves, the former representing individual thought processes, moral wiring (rectitude) and idiosyncrasies; the latter a manifestation of what others see in and think about you. A very interesting corollary to this manifestation would be akin to what the French existentialist Jean Paul Sartre illustrated in his narrative of "*The Look*" in the *Encounter with the Other*. In it, Sartre explains a situation where an individual makes an awkward or vulgar gesture only to discover with shock that someone has seen him. The sudden realization of the vulgarity of the act elicits shame, but it is a shame that is not reflective on me (the individual), but rather on the presence of another in my isolated consciousness. As the *Other* becomes an indispensable mediator between *myself* and *me*, I am only ashamed of myself as I appear to the *Other*. My appearance is a "mode of consciousness which seem (even while remaining strictly in for-itself) to point to a radically different type of ontological structure which happens to be mine. I am thus, only concerned about myself, and yet this concern for-myself reveals to me a being which is *my* being without being-for-me" (Sartre, 1965, pp. 188–189). Due to the fact that *being* can only be what the *Other* makes of me, the individual experiences we have with others may reveal a lot more about us and who we are. This is the inner consciousness reflected in and born out of the tension between what others see and think about you and what you want them to see and think about you. Because the individual is both the cause and effect of this tension, its resolution becomes a crucial pathway through which he is able to reveal himself to the world outside of himself.

The Social Environment

The social environment of citizenship exists as a subculture somewhat distinct from the individual while he also remains part of it. Family, friends, neighbors and society make up the social environment within which citizenship can be expressed. Social clubs and community associations help to reinforce cultural norms, traditions, civic obligations and community service in the collective interest. Although an individual can still express certain measures of autonomy, freedom and judgment, his position as a free moral agent is limited to those exercises of right that do not infringe on the rights of others. Free expression in this regard is confined and limited by the prevailing social and political conventions as well as the boundaries of the law.

Social citizenship also imposes an obligation on the state to initiate such measures as may be necessary to afford each and every citizen the opportunity to secure the basic necessities of life and subsistence, especially in matters resulting from structural dislocations often associated with liberal capitalist economies. It was in this regard's that T.H. Marshall recognized "social citizenship rights as a dimension of the full and complex status of citizenship, and argued that this, in turn, had been achieved in the context of the historical development of modern democratic-capitalist welfare states" (Roche, 2002, p. 76). There is a basic expectation that each individual in society will abide by the existing rules of reciprocity in the sharing and use of communal property and in the exercise of collective rights in the public interest. It is a recognition that you share the road with others that prevents you from willfully blocking it with a car; it is recognizing how other users might feel that keeps one from parking in reserved spaces not meant for them or parking in designated handicapped spaces. By obeying these social conventions, one gives life to the ideal of social citizenship.

Social citizenship draws upon the role of the individual as a member of society in which communal relationships are tied to social interactions on various issues concerning the democratic discourse—issues such as the economy, taxes, unemployment, health care, inflation, ideological differences, electoral politics, democracy and those related to quality of life. In his *Bowling Alone: America's Declining Social Capital*, Robert D. Putnam (1995a) bemoans the declining level of electoral participation, civic and community engagement and membership in neighborhood organizations as result of an increasing loss of *social capital* in America. Putnam's (1993) seminal work on the topic of local governments in Italy concluded that the performance of government and other social institutions is powerfully influenced by citizen engagement in community affairs. By social capital he means features of social life-networks, norms and trust that enable participants to act together more effectively to pursue shared objectives. "To the extent that the norms, networks, and trust link substantial sectors of the community and 'bridge' underlying social cleavages, then the enhanced cooperation is likely to serve broader interests and to be widely welcomed" (Putnam, 1995b, pp. 664–684). He was therefore concerned that the absence of shared values, ideas and common aspirations critical to the validation and sustenance of the civic republican traditions that the Founders had envisaged would be inimical to and consequential for the preservation of enduring democracies.

The Professional Environment

The professional environment of citizenship involves the role of individuals in their professions and when engaged in the world of work, in either the private or public sectors. As illustrated by Max Weber (1998, p. 43), we understand citizenship in this category (though not exclusively) to be "those 'persons of property and culture,' entrepreneurs, recipients of funded incomes, and in general all persons of academic culture, a certain class standard of living, and a certain social prestige." In this regard, the proposition is that a citizen can operate in multiple environments at the same time, one primary and the other(s) secondary. The professional-in-office is a representative citizen encumbered by three sets of obligations: to the profession, to the agency or organization and to the dominant regime values broadly shared and understood by members of the political community. Professional and career public servants are the bridge between what the government does about the problems and needs of the citizenry and how the public appraises the government's effort in addressing them. It is therefore incumbent on the public servant to serve as well as "enhance the knowledge base of public affairs so that citizens can understand how real public affairs operate, how practical problems affect public affairs, and what the criteria are by which options are judged" (McGregor, 1984, p. 130).

Because every public action can be judged in terms of its consequences for citizenship, public servants and politicians do not cease to be ordinary citizens when they hold public office (van Gunsteren, 1988, p. 735). The issue of value dichotomy is considered in light of the professional as *bureaucrat-in-government* and the professional as *citizen-in-the public* (society), "but like every other person, the citizen-in-public is also influenced by the interaction of the political, cultural, social and economic values of society" (Kalu, 2003b, p. 550). As a bureaucrat in government, the professional is equally influenced by the broader socio-political value system and the more specific and narrow value orientation of the individual's organizational culture and administrative responsibilities. How effectively the individual bridges the similarities and contrasts of these two value domains goes a long way in determining to what extent the professional attains the status of a virtuous citizen. Cicero (1913) echoes the same in his *De Officiis*, pointing out that while some virtues are rooted in one's persona as a human being subject to natural laws, others find expression in the specific roles individuals occupy as well as the existing customs of the city.

As David K. Hart (1984, pp. 116–117) would also argue, "when one accepts the calling of public administrator (servant), one also accepts the responsibility of transcending that ordinary virtue to seek honor; and the cultivation of honor and superior prudence is the *sine qua non* of professional responsibility." Hence, "the exercise of citizenship as the public office of the individual must carry with it an obligation to consider individual and group interests in the context of larger social and community interests" (Cooper, 1984, p. 147). The professional calling requires public servants to be virtuous citizens as well as honorable bureaucrats (Hart, 1984) and to commit to the common project of securing the public good and seeking excellence, probity and civic virtue in the execution of their respective functions.

Toward Citizenship: A Theoretical Postscript

It is important that we continue to explore how we theorize on the subject matter of citizenship, its relevance in the world we live and how it helps to address competing issues of the human condition. Can citizenship help to bridge conflicts between and within nationalities, states, cultures and religions, as well as in inter-state politics? Can the ideal and practice of citizenship be used to narrow or eliminate multiple cleavages that separate people of different geopolitical persuasions and help build a future world premised on reason, humaneness and collective interest? The many different strands of citizenship create a double-edged sword. On the one hand they may help to foster an exciting body of literature and intellectual richness, but on the other they create a confusing maze of epistemological double-talks that causes us to use a great deal of time in a fruitless attempt to unravel.

My observation is that in exploring the emerging literature on citizenship, we are doing the same things we have been doing since the symposium on *Citizenship and Public Administration* published as a Special Issue in the *Public Administration Review* of March 1984. We are still drawn to the perennial construction of fanciful terms, romanticized and buzz-infused metaphors and esoteric catchphrases in conceptualization and elaboration. The multiple conceptualizations we have come to apply to the construct make it quite difficult to appreciate or validate the true essence of the term and to come to a consensus on its multidimensionality or lack thereof. Instead, we have unfortunately become victims of our own self-induced intellectual hubris. Why do we need to choose between civic republican and liberal political virtues? Why must we choose differentiated as opposed to multicultural citizenship or its variants in communitarianism, cosmopolitanism and republican citizenship?

We have tried variously to conceive of citizenship "as an expression of historically specific and historically variable relationships" (Walker, 1999, p. 172), a mark of pride and achievement (Walker, 1999, p. 108), status and activity (Kymlicka and Norman, 1995, p. 284), man of virtue, honor and prudence (Hart, 1984), office in a historical community (van Gunsteren, 1988, p. 735), distribution of authority (Flathman, 1981), political status between legal and ethical roles (Lowi, 1981), man in society (Mosher, 1941), interaction between ethical and legal dimensions (Long, 1981), supportive and committed (Sniderman, 1981), high ethical dimension (Cooper, 1984), rights and obligation (Kalu, 2003a) and substantive ethical citizenship grounded in *elenchic* inquiry (Ventriss, 2007). But as in all other historical facts, some of these simultaneously carry with them the ambivalence of a human condition caught between relative autonomy and resigned indignation on the one hand, and cautious optimism and melancholy, on the other.

Accepting the fact that the ideal of citizenship may be reflected as a multidimensional construct, the simple reality of the matter, despite arguments to the contrary, is that it does exist. A starting point therefore would be to focus on the *practice* and *experience* of citizenship, not on its definition. If we are still not sure what the ideal stands for, we can construct it by attaching meaning to the various processes commonly associated with citizenship as activity. But what we seem to have missed in all the various iterations is the fact that there is a common thread that runs through them: citizenship as status, rights and obligation. If we can use these common denominators as starting points, it is possible that we will discover that many of the other attributes are mere derivatives that can easily be accommodated within the three major strands already indicated.

2 Classical Orthodoxy

Greco-Roman Heritage

To understand the potential of citizenship, what it is and what it could become, we must know its history and understand what it meant for people before us.

(van Gunsteren, 1998, p. 11)

Ideas about human nature and its relationship to the cosmic universe have generally come from an attempt to understand the principles and methods for which matter, form, time, body and soul serve their respective functions. Knowledge can be built from intuition, experience or general assumptions about the behavior of complex and simple phenomena in both time and space; suffice it therefore to say that ideas can come from anywhere. The notion of citizenship—as we generally conceive of it today—"is a derivative of the emergence of the nation-state, which, in turn, was a direct outgrowth of the medieval period" (Gawthrop and Waldo, 1984, p. 101). "Citizenship was a meaningful concept in the Greco-Roman period, but from roughly the 5th to the 6th centuries—from the fall of the Roman Empire; from the triumph of Christianity over classical paganism to the revolt of Protestantism against Catholic Christianity" (Hearnshaw, 1981, p. 19). "the idea of citizenship evolved into that which clearly resembles a transcendent ethics of noble civility" (Gawthrop and Waldo, 1984, p. 101). Because it "implied a close union with the ancestral soil and worship in the ancestral religion, these became the exclusive bonds with which communities were knitted together; and which, in their exclusivity, denied the alien and stranger full rights of participation" (Gorman, 1992, p. 6).

Aside from its origins and early intellectual history drawn from Greek and Roman republicanism, the current ideology of citizenship saw its more profound expression in the early modern era and during the French Revolution. "In its Jacobian phase, the revolution is best understood as an effort to establish citizenship as the dominant identity of every Frenchman—against the alternative identities of religion, estate, family, and region; hence citizenship was to replace religious faith and familial loyalty as the central motive of virtuous conduct" (Walzer, 1989, p. 211). Key theorists were Machiavelli, Harrington, Montesquieu and Mably, but it was Rousseau and later Kant who gave citizenship its modern philosophical grounding, connecting it to the theory of consent, liberty and obedience (Walzer, 1989, p. 212). Today, modern expressions of citizenship remain contested, involving but not limited to references to nobility of spirit, honor, civic virtue, community, entitlements, compassion, independence and autonomy.

Of Philosophy and the Cosmos

Evidently, many of the classical thinkers of antiquity were of Greek and Roman origin and discussed very complex issues regarding human nature and the universe, as well as the role of man in it. They sought to address ontological and empirical questions surrounding objects, function, life, causality and essence, as well as such issues as happiness, love, friendship, virtue and vice. "The Greeks' concern with immortality grew out of their experience of an immortal nature and immortal gods which together surrounded the individual lives of men; hence embedded in a cosmos where everything was immortal, mortality became the hallmark of human existence" (Arendt, 1958, p. 18). It was from this train of thought and ontological reflections that later thinkers drew inspiration: from the Cartesian rationalism of René Descartes, the rationalism of Spinoza, the mathematical canons of Leibniz, the classical liberalism of Locke, the empiricism of Hobbes and Hume, the political realism of Machiavelli, the existentialism of Nietzsche, the utilitarianism of Bentham and Mill, the pragmatism of Dewey and the absurdism of Camus to the more contemporary thinkers like Heidegger, Rawls, Derrida, Rorty, Walzer and Sandel. One can rarely read a major work in philosophy without coming across one or two verses drawn from one of the Greco-Roman predecessors, verses that also delineate political thinking and critical views on such issues as justice, obligation, equality, ethics, politics and citizenship.

Among the early Greek philosophers were the Milesian Monists, the iconoclast Heraclitus, the Sophists, Plato, Aristotle, Epicurus and Zeno the Stoic. One of the most prominent of the Milesian monists was Anaximenes whose main argument was that everything about nature evolves from air. It is for him "boundless and unlimited air, out of which comes to be things that come to be, and things that will be, including the gods and divine things" (Reeve and Miller, 2006, p. 3), but the iconoclast Heraclitus views the cosmos as stasis in movement, harmony in opposition and creativity in strife. There is a divine *logos* (logic) within which the cosmos operates, and all movements in this regard are designed by nature for specific purposes in accordance with which all other things follow. Contemporary political theory drew heavily from Plato's *The Republic* on such issues as the social division of roles in the ideal state, issues of justice, the nature of God, philosophical education, rules of war and the duality of human nature (soul and body). It is from the *Symposium* and the *Dialogues*, particularly the *Euthyphro*, the *Apology* and the *Phaedo*, that much about Socrates' life and philosophical method is gleaned, since he, as much as can be surmised, left no written works of his own.

In as much as Socrates' philosophical citizenship relies on a person's powers of independent reasoning and judgment, Aristotle draws on crucial lessons about citizenship in the context of political participation, civic virtue and the common good of the community. Reflecting on *The Politics*, one could infer that while he may have been inclined to think of the citizen as a kind of species and to look for the marks by which it may be recognized, "his criterion for excellence in a political arrangement is that people involved should be enabled by that arrangement, to choose to function well and to lead a flourishing life, to the extent that the polity's material and natural circumstances permit" (Nussbaum, 1990, p.208). The Epicureans were not given to the Aristotelian emphasis on political participation, but for them virtue stemmed from the community of friendships or relationships one developed in life, as one could rely on these for security, happiness and the good life. The Stoics, particularly Zeno and his successor Chrysippus, argued that one should dutifully participate in politics as long as something did not prevent this, because politics is part of nature's plan for human happiness (divine providence) and hence is consistent with the natural law by which human conduct is harmonized with the cosmic order.

Roman political philosophy drew equally from Epicureanism and Stoicism, but with some fundamental differences in application and moderation. In addition to Boethius' *The Consolations of Philosophy,* which depicts a teleological ascent to the knowledge of God and the roles of fortune, patience and wisdom in addressing some of life's most difficult and enduring questions, works by Cicero, Lucretius, Seneca, Epictetus, Marcus Aurelius, Sextus Empiricus and the later Neoplatonist Plotinus had classical Greek influences. Cicero's writings had an enormous influence on the philosophical education of Rome and much of European civilization in the areas of law, logic, oratory, citizenship and republican politics. Besides his civil defense of individuals in legal matters, he wrote and delivered speeches against political authoritarianism and the rise of dictatorship and misgovernment in republican Rome. Among these were *The Verrine Orations* (delivered against Gaius Verres, governor of the province of Sicily), *In Catilinam* (a political tirade delivered against Lucius Sergius Catilina following what became known as the Catilinarian conspiracy to overthrow the Roman republic) and the *Philippics* (against Marc Antony and the Triumvirate). There were also philosophical treatises such as the *Tusculan Disputations* and his *Letters to Atticus*. His three books, which exercised enormous influence on the development of contemporary Western moral and political thought, were *De re publica* (*On the Commonwealth*—an assemblage of people associated with one another by agreement on law and community of interest), *De legibus* (*On the Laws*) and *De officiis* (*On Duties*—his work on political morality and the republic). Collectively, these works have endured and remain influential in shaping contemporary political thinking and governance. They also provide us with critical information for our knowledge and understanding of the period as well as the framework of Roman politics, society and citizenship.

The Family Structure and Relationships

The ideal of citizenship has always been at the center of classical thought, both in matters of membership in the political community and individual roles and obligations within it. The Socratic quest for truth and the good life were meant to suggest a crucial element of citizenship—that the *telos* of any political community is that of a life of consistent inquiry that transcends virtue and a good life lived dutifully for the self and for others. Life in early Hellenic society revolved around the family structure, and membership in the family was based on marriage, birth and status. Within the makeup of each family, one would expect to see three elements: a male, female and servant, each playing a different functional and leadership role. Even in a master-servant relationship, a strong bond of allegiance existed among members of ancient Greek families.

The Greeks of the time of Homer lived under a social system in which property relations determined not only the economic bases of society, but also marriage and all other phases of development. The dogged appreciation of the value of higher civilization's simpler gifts created a general desire to possess the more complicated products and facilities. The result was that self-interest, vanity, love of beauty and other elemental passions aroused in the average Greek the desire to assimilate what might aid him in the struggle for existence and the expression of individuality (Keller, 1902, p. 7). The nature of social stratification in the public sphere also found general expression in the household. Women were not considered the equals of men and, in fact, were viewed as, and expected to be, managers of household affairs including the servants and slaves. Marriage was entered into in order to have offspring and for dynastic and lineage reasons.

Because "the system consisted in the superposition of a patriarchal family upon a group of inferiors, traditions of monarchy were strong among the Homeric Greeks; and to them, monarchy was a symbol of culture and good discipline" (Keller, 1902, p. 251). This provided the leadership, military skill, valor and decisiveness needed in times of war and violence. In this regard, they detested the rule of the many, what eventually evolved into the idea of *demokratia.* The king had considerable direct power over the life of the people. As Keller (1902) points out, social class among the Homeric Greeks was based on a ranking order from the highest to the lowest in terms of king, nobles, *hetairoi* (King's elite cavalry), people and slaves. While the heads of noble families were represented in the circle of the *gerontes,* which surrounded the king, age was also respected as it was seen as the abode of education and knowledge. Over time, intermarriage among citizens and the assimilation of languages, customs, religions and mores tended to narrow class differences and create a greater sense of community.

Despite slight variations from the Homeric world of the individual hero in which a strong powerful leader was responsible for the family (*oikos*), in "the *polis* communities of old Greece, the ancestor's land and their tombs which, invariably, were the customary evidence of their ancient ownership and the object of the family's cult, provided strong unifying bonds within which the individual lived as a member of his family" (Lacey, 1968, p. 16). "The spirit of unity and civic consciousness was rooted in *oikoi* (lands and houses) and cults that the families felt had been vested in them by right of descent from some mythical, heroic founder" (Lacey, 1968, p. 19). The family institution thus became the bedrock of nobility and the source of upward mobility into the ruling political hierarchy.

As illustrated by W.K. Lacey (1968, pp. 20–21), the age of the Sophists (comprising the last half of the fifth century) who arrived on mainland Greece and Athens from the Aegean and western Greek worlds sought to challenge the old accepted code of behavior and values—thereby shattering the unifying family bond that facilitated membership, tradition and loyalty within Greek society. While this development may have set in motion the divisive effects that led to the Peloponnesian War (431–404), it may also have led to the rise of greater individualism that extended up to the Hellenic Age. Because of the greater freedom of action for individuals in relation to their families, there developed a much lesser sense of responsibility toward the family (*oikos*) as well as the state (*polis*).

To the extent that "the family as an independent unit sustained the relationship between free members of society, it was also a constituent unit of a much larger unit out of which the city-state or *polis* evolved" (Lacey, 1968, p. 21). With the family structure integrally built into the structure of the state and to the extent that each harbored elements of the other, early Greeks viewed outsiders as foreigners, barbarians and slaves, since none of them qualified for the conferment of citizenship status. Natural and mineral resources were considered community property, and the rights to mine and harvest them were granted only to citizens. This attitude was quite prevalent, especially in Athens "where the bulk of the population was made up of slaves and resident foreigners, and where illegitimate offspring were legion" (Werner, 1977, p. 5).

Furthermore, the element of disunity was also facilitated as a result of the natural environment and the location of the various communities. The geographical spread of the Greek islands and the sea distances between them made it possible for local interests to triumph over those of the states, thus making control and accountability more difficult. To "prevent wars and to promote regional security, it became necessary for neighboring and more or less kindred communities to form defense leagues (such as in *Phokis* and *Boiotia*) for mutual protection and as a deterrence against wars between them" (Burn, 1965, p. 65). As Eric Voegelin (1957, p. 118) points out, the fundamental problem of early Hellenic politics was the inability to overcome the gentilician (tribal) cohesion and to create political institutions on a regional or national scale. Because the *polis* was constructed out of families and tribes, no direct membership in the *polis* was possible since citizenship in Athens could be acquired through birth or through adoption into one of the *phratries* (kinship groups) or *demes* (one of the local government units inhabited by the same tribe). Due to the simple fact that the idea of citizenship required specific sets of commonalities that foreigners or barbarians do not share with the others, the issue of membership and the criteria for achieving and sustaining it became paramount.

Civic Education and Political Life

Similarly, early Roman society was based on the family, and economic life was built around it. As described in Lionel Casson's *Everyday Life in Ancient Rome* (1998, pp. 10–17), while the head of the family was not necessarily a Homeric hero, he was the oldest male offspring in the family lineage and was popularly known as *paterfamilias* (father of the family). Marriages were generally arranged as a means of carrying on a family's name and protecting its property. Beyond the characteristic childhood plays and ceremonies, education was enforced very early in the life of the Roman child. Nurses accompanied the girls to school, and special slaves known as *paedagogi* or 'child-leaders' took the boys. Special education lasted up to 14 years of age and involved pedagogy in grammar, syntax and literature in both Latin and Greek. The curriculum included studies of Homer, Aeschylus, Sophocles, Euripides, Menander, Vergil, and Horace. As in Greece, "the purpose of education is to produce a good man, the necessary framework on which to shape a good citizen" (Heater, 1999, p. 66); and in accordance with Aristotle's (1948) admonition that the citizens of a state should always be educated to suit the constitutions of their state—as a means of cultivating the kind of civic virtue necessary for the good life.

Early Roman society was made up of a combination of educated and wealthy aristocracy/patricians, plebeians, a limited middle class and the peasantry whose toil was mostly in agriculture and farming. But as people migrated to the cities, Rome in particular, a domiciled upper-class strata began to emerge as other cities, again like Rome, assumed more cosmopolitan characteristics. Foreigners (*peregrini*) were not entitled to or granted Roman citizenship "except by decree of the Senate under the Republic or by individual grant of the Emperor" (Balsdon, 1979, p. 13). However, foreigners who excelled in battle on the side of the Romans were sometimes gifted with Roman citizenship as when Pompey bestowed it upon Theophanes of Mitylene "who from being his expert adviser on eastern affairs in his campaign in the eastern Mediterranean, became his most effective adjutant in Rome" (Balsdon, 1979, p. 83). To become a Roman was very much cherished, and being granted Roman citizenship was an occasion for celebration and an entry into a life of opportunity, at least for most of them.

Aside from being a native-born Roman, there were institutional mechanisms for accession to citizenship. Among these were as a result of change in the status of old towns or that of newly-found communities; a resident of any Roman colony who eventually registered in the colony census or for legal service in the magistracy; a foreigner, volunteer or slave who served in any of the armed forces; a slave who was freed with the proper formalities; a petitioner who submitted *libelli* (certificates of sacrifice) to the Emperor in consultation with his Privy Council; and an allied soldier fighting on behalf of Rome (Balsdon, 1979, pp. 83–91). It was difficult for the emancipated former slave to share in the benefits of Roman citizenship. "While various careers open to the freeborn Roman were closed to him, he could not, even under the right age, volunteer for service in the legions or in the Praetorian Guard; and except in Caesar's colonies, he could not be a town-councilor or a magistrate" (Balsdon, 1979, p. 92). Former slaves hardly shared in the political and economic life of Rome.

The Political and Cultural Context

What classical Greece and Rome shared was a form of significant and sustained participation in the political life of the community. For the Greeks, it was a matter of being a free native-born, property owner, and there was a general bias toward male patriarchy. Citizenship was defined by lineage or genealogy, social class distinctions and oftentimes military service and was limited to those who could actually have a share in governing (Chandler, 1984, p. 201) or the "right of sharing in deliberative or judicial office" (Bellamy, 2008, p. 32). Because most public offices were chosen by lot and usually held for one or two years, the aim was to increase the likelihood that all citizens would have an equal chance of exercising political power; hence, there were no career politicians (Bellamy, 2008, pp. 32–33). Yet citizenship in Athens was a fairly full-time occupation, one that offered limited opportunity for the development of private interests. It was also one that excluded women, children, the aged, foreigners and slaves.

But for ancient Rome, "citizenship was understood in reference to legal standards of equality (*jus gentium*) premised on justice, common sense, and fair dealing; but one which undermined rigid distinctions between citizens and foreigner while embracing citizenship in terms of a community of civic friendship" (Chandler, 1984, p. 201). To the extent that "the state is the *affairs* of the people (*res publica*), the Romans were also of the view that it cannot exist permanently unless it recognizes the mutual obligations and rights that binds its citizens together" (Chandler, 1984, p. 201). While the Greeks relied on categorical equality, the Roman political culture preferred universal equality under the law for all citizens as the most effective means for granting rights, as well as serving particular interests that sustained and enhanced civic life in the republic.

The real difference in the Greek and Roman disposition toward civic political participation is a matter of degree and, in most cases, substance. As pointed out by Richard Bellamy (2008, p. 36), despite being able to vote and become Tribunes and magistrates, Roman citizens never possessed the same degree of political influence as their Athenian counterparts. Rather, the version of Roman citizenship given was of a legal rather than political kind—'*civitas sine suffragio*' (citizenship without the vote)—since the ultimate power of decision making rested with the Senate, essentially dominated by patricians in both the magistracy and the consulships (Bellamy, 2008, p. 39).

For the Romans, civic virtue, and the prerogative of political participation, was not necessarily a moral question, but was premised on exploits and chivalry in military service and in serving other requirements of state. While both aspects required performances of one kind or another, they nonetheless were opposites. Roman citizenship was not something to be accorded without careful consideration to aliens, but as the empire grew, citizenship extended more broadly (Gorman, 1992, p. 13). The two essential obligations of Roman citizens were to pay one's taxes and to serve in the army, and although active political participation was not demanded, the state was obliged to protect their rights even as these varied over time and among different classes of citizens (Gorman, 1992, p. 13). It is thus possible to suggest that the additional guarantee of civil liberties for Roman citizens was an early indication of the reciprocal nature of obligation and the specific role of the state.

Republican Citizenship and Aristotelian Moral Imperative

It would be a gross understatement to suggest that much of Aristotle's political morality was anchored in considerations of the relationship (or rather coexistence) among the *polis* (community/state), the *polites* (citizens) and *politeia* (the constitution). Due to the simple fact that he grants primacy to the citizen in relation to the state, it behooves us to consider whether the state should be obligated to the citizen, rather than the other way around. When we say that "a citizen is a member of a city, we are also asking the question as to what constitutes membership of a city?" (Aristotle, 1962, p. 104). In Book III of *The Politics*, Aristotle defines a citizen as one who participates in judgment and "officially determined authority," that is, holding legal, political, or administrative office—a definition he considers more applicable to democracy than all other forms of government. For him, "citizen" is a species with distinct and recognizable marks, a particular class of men to which no one who is constantly engaged in commercial or manual labor can possibly belong. In this particular case, Plato's laborer class would not belong; perhaps the guardians would, but not the slaves or youth because they are not yet mature enough to make a reasonable contribution to the welfare of the *polis*.

But "as soon as a man becomes entitled (by carrying out some deserved act) to participate in authority, deliberative or judicial, we deem him to be a citizen of that state" (Aristotle, 1962, p. 104). Aristotle's argument focuses on the functional and instrumental aspects of citizenship and essentially negates issues of rights. When he talks about entitlement, he discusses it as a status that is conferred *in lieu of*, that is, after one has done something to contribute to the general welfare of the community. In the Aristotelian republic, one's citizenship is relative to some concrete or "thick" measurement. The criterion of measurement is the extent of an individual's participation in the community or state but in such a way that participation enhances the good life for all members (citizens) of the community. To the extent that active participation in the *polis* exonerates one's citizenship status, all considerations of citizenship must be made in lieu of the *polis*. The *polis* is a universal community, whereas citizenship reflects a universal activity; and to construct a good *polis* we need citizens who have the rational ability to control their passions and appetites. Because the law helps to impart virtue on the citizens, the project of the *polis* becomes one of human flourishing and virtue.

In his *Outline of a Theory of Citizenship*, Bryan Turner (1990, p. 193) argues that a theory of citizenship must also produce a theory of the state. He points out that the state provides the principal element in the maintenance and development of social rights, as it is the political instrument through which political movements seek redress of their circumstances by the legitimization of their claims against society. While the idea of claims implies an expression of rights, the issue that Aristotelian republicanism raises is how these rights become legitimate or authenticated, that is, granted some fundamental remedies backed by law. In an Aristotelian world, the criteria for guaranteeing citizenship rights include wealth, property and political participation. The state exists for noble actions: "Those who do noble deeds are contributing to the quality of political association; and those who contribute most are entitled to a larger share than those who, though they may be equal or even superior in birth and family, but are inferior in noble deeds and so in the essential goodness they bring to the polis" (Aristotle, 1962, p. 121).

For Aristotle, the instrumentality of one's participation and contribution to the good life in the *polis* confers authentic citizenship, not as a matter of right but as a matter of doing that which brings the highest good for the community. It is a matter of being conscientiously drawn to the ideal of 'ruling and being ruled in turn.' While he agreed that the nature of participation depends on the type of *politeia* that exists between the people and the state, he maintains that a certain level of superiority or nobility of action on the individual's part is a prerequisite for any claim to public office and privilege. Among the prerequisites are good birth and ownership of property, moral qualities (virtue), justice, courage and a high level of culture and education. "Men are not equal in these respects and any state which ignores this fact and thinks in terms of absolute equality must be one of the wrong types of deviations—wrong types of constitutions" (Aristotle, 1962, p. 127).

Like Plato before him, Aristotle recognizes and accepts that there is inequality in nature and that any state that aims to satisfy the essential purpose of providing the good life must recognize this inequality. To the extent that states are different, we can therefore expect their conceptions of equality, fairness and justice to be different because these are relative to each given context and for the persons concerned. The missing link here is that Aristotle does not consider equality, justice or fairness in the practical sense of according to each the same amount of goodness that has been accorded to others. For him, these normative values—though worthy of pursuit by any responsible state—are relative based on individual capabilities as permitted by natural possibilities. Therefore, if we embrace the Aristotelian conception of citizenship we invariably, must also embrace the implied inequality.

The liberal argues that citizens have been treated as free and equal if they have been given equal amounts of all-purpose resources (Dworkin, 1981) or if inequalities can be justified as being for the good of the worst off (Rawls, 1971). On the other hand, Aristotelians "hold that citizens have been treated as free only if they have been given the necessary conditions for the exercise of choice and practical reason—among which will be education, political participation, and the absence of degrading labor" (Nussbaum, 1990, p. 216). They have been treated as equals only if the whole of each life has been considered with rich imagination (Nussbaum and Sen, 1989) and each person has been given whatever he or she needs to be in a position to live a rich and fully human life, up to the limit permitted by nature (Nussbaum, 1990, p. 217).

Following Aristotle, Rousseau and John Stuart Mill, many modern philosophers assume that political participation itself will teach people responsibility and tolerance. They place their fate in the activity of participation as the means whereby individuals become accustomed to the duties of citizenship. They believe that as political participation enlarges the minds of individuals and familiarizes them with interests that lie beyond the immediacy of personal circumstances and environment, they will acknowledge that public concerns should be given attention (Oldfield, 1990). However, in light of the political realities of the modern state, political participation can hardly be taken for granted as a universally binding or desirable axiom. Political participation can be a result of the scope or nature of political or civil liberties granted to the citizens by the state. When these liberties are circumscribed—say, in an oligarchy, dictatorship or other forms of authoritarian systems or where severe discriminatory practices have become institutionalized—the vigorous exercise of political participation as a condition of authentic citizenship is thus reduced to irrelevance.

Civic Virtue as Political Morality

The issue of virtue is central to the ideals of Aristotelian civic republicanism. Aristotle seeks to be the rational voice of the best citizens of the best city-state; he holds that the city-state is the unique political form in which the virtues of human life can be genuinely and fully exhibited. Human beings, like members of all other species, have a specific nature such that they have certain aims and goals and move by nature toward a specific *telos*. Every activity, every inquiry, every practice aims at some good—that at which humans characteristically aim. For Aristotle, this is the "good" that is located in and partially defined by the characteristics of the *polis* and yet is also cosmic and universal. He calls it *eudaimonia*-blessedness, happiness and prosperity. What constitutes "the good" for man is a complete human life lived at its best, and the exercise of the virtues is a necessary and central part of such a life, not a mere preparatory exercise to secure such a life. Therefore, one can expect the immediate outcome of the exercise of virtue to be a choice that issues in the right action. It is the correctness of the end of the purposive choice that virtue causes. Taken together, virtues are dispositions not only to act in particular ways, but also to feel in particular ways. To act virtuously is not to act against inclination; it is to act from inclination formed by the cultivation of virtues. Intellectual virtues are acquired through teaching and the virtues of character from habitual exercise. Virtue is a partnership of ruling and being ruled with others who must be equally as morally autonomous (Cooper, 1984, p. 143). Therefore, each individual must act as an independent and responsible moral agent.

Aristotle seems to consider "goodness" and "virtue" in functional or instrumental terms, in terms of "what I can do," not "what I am." The American Founders were familiar with Aristotle's argument that the "good man" and the "good citizen" are not necessarily the same, except in the ideal state; but they also understood his view that virtue—oral and intellectual ability—is a quality that is always needed for the exercise of power. The Founders were also receptive to the idea of moral individualism because they "understood that the key to a successful democracy lay more in the quality of the citizens than in the quality of their leaders" (Hart, 1984, p. 114).

As Hart (1984, p. 114) argues, "the primary responsibility of the virtuous citizen is to ascertain the truth about the moral nature of the individual, to assimilate that truth to one's self (one's goodness), and then to cast it in terms of one's civic life (the goodness of the *polis*)." By "swearing" an oath to serve the United States and its citizens (an act of choice), the Constitution imposes an administrative imperative on public bureaucrats—to preserve the norms of the state and the values upon which it was built, to ensure equality of opportunity for all, meritocracy in service, due process, punishment conditional on intent, fairness and equity, public accountability and political responsiveness. Virtue in the administrative context transcends civility, forbearance, moral philosophy and, above all, a belief in the regime values and the relative obligations they entail. To the extent that policy makers and administrators embody the regime values-in-action, they become moral agents in the mutual encounter between bureaucrats and the citizenry. Hence, "we must seek virtue in our citizens and honor in our bureaucrats" (Hart, 1984, p. 114).

Critical Republicanism: A Retrospective

The ancient republican tradition of Greece and Rome saw political participation, though in different variations, as a means of contributing to the welfare of the state. But in the Aristotelian state, it becomes more problematic when wealth and property are used as determinants for political participation and when inequalities are accepted as a matter of fact, as long as everyone has a fundamental equality of opportunity. Aristotle was concerned about the nature of distributive justice in terms of political offices and rewards based on a recognition of excellence; yet, given an ideology of personal achievement among liberal democracies, the equalization of educational opportunities, for example, may give all children a basic education but would not eradicate inequality of outcomes in a situation that emphasized competitiveness and personal aspiration" (Turner, 1986, 114). Hence, any emphasis on the doctrine of equality of opportunity must be measured against the reciprocal backdrop of equality of outcomes.

But that would be less of a concern for Aristotle, particularly for a well-ordered society. For him, politics is about forming character, civic virtue and the realization of the good life, but not about economic rewards; therefore the institutions of the state should be directed toward these ends. As free moral agents, individuals can seek the fullest expression of liberty and independence in freedom of thought, but then these rights must be considered in lieu of competing rights of other individuals as well as those of the state. In this sense, and for the individual and the *polis*, any expression of rights and freedom is always contingent. The contingency is based on the two principles of self-restraint (discipline) and collective self-regard (a concern for the goodness of the community). These, therefore, serve as necessary ingredients critical to attaining the virtuous life, goodness, and citizenship both in the private and public spheres.

3 Citizenship in the Liberal State

How Benign?

The Treaty of Westphalia (1648) introduced the modern state system as a primary institution in interstate relations, an institution endowed with the principles of sovereignty and territorial integrity over its geographical and domestic affairs. It was a major shift in world order, one that brought about legal equality and increasing secularism within and between the states. It was a treaty of mutual and peaceful co-existence but one that did not go far in deciding how each state would organize internally with respect to the grants of specific freedoms, rights and responsibilities. It was left to each state to decide for itself the type and character of government it wanted, be it monarchy, aristocracy or democracy. As Pierre Beaudry (2003) points out, the treaty only succeeded because of an economic policy of protectionism and directed public credit dirigisme—aimed to create sovereign nation-states and designed by France's Cardinal Jules Mazarin and his great protégé Jean-Baptiste Colbert.

Just as Mazarin's and Colbert's common-good principle of the 'Advantage of the Other' triumphed over the imperial designs of both France's Louis XIV himself and the Venetian-controlled Hapsburg Empire, the same principle brought in the eighteenth century similar ideals of Leibniz and Locke in shaping the American republic's founding documents—the victory of 'the pursuit of happiness' and the Lockean principle of 'life, liberty, and property' (Beaudry, 2003). These value objectives have shaped the emergence and durability of the liberal state in contemporary national and interstate relations. According to J.G.A. Pocock (1975, p. 462), "the American founders occupied a Machiavellian Moment—a crisis in the relations between personality and society, virtue and corruption—but at the same time stood at a moment in history when that problem was being either left behind or admitted insoluble." By contrast, in the liberal order, government is segregated from society in order to serve it. One such control is transformed citizenship, where citizen is no longer the role you play in government but the role you occupy in the gap that has been created between society and government. While voting and advocacy—the primary mediating activities of liberal citizenship—are important, they constitute a complete definition of citizenship in neither theory nor practice (Racine, 1995, p. 446). They only reflect, in the Aristotelian tradition, the participatory or political aspects of citizenship.

The ideal underlying citizenship in the modern liberal state is increasingly one of equality in principle, doubtless in fact, but that provides legitimate reason for citizens to invoke specific rights claims against the state. Idealistically, liberals have historically sought to create the "conditions for the application of reason that maximizes individual freedom coupled with responsiveness and responsibility to others—as a means of securing a public framework of caring and equality that transcends existing social, political and economic boundaries" (Raskin, 2004, p. 12). For most liberals, "the modern liberal state meant changing the nature of democracy and even the republic into a system of rule for the many rather than rule over the many" (Raskin, 2004, p. 13), but conservatives argue that the tenets of liberal permissiveness and radical individualism have led to a multiplicity of rights claims and social decay that comes without the promise of happiness (Raskin, 2004, p. 12).

It becomes problematic when one has to re-earn those rights by engaging in acts that accord primacy to the interest of the state or community. In this particular case, the idea of equality and the concept of rights become conditional, some citizens having more than others. While all citizens retain their basic constitutional rights (that is, civil liberties as granted in the Bill of Rights), the structure of society engenders a level of functional inequality that opens up possibilities for some to excel more than the rest and in many fundamental ways. I propose that in liberal societies, two strands of citizenship explain this phenomenon: normative and instrumental citizenship (Table 3.1).

Normative citizenship is driven by natural law and encapsulated in the political and constitutional origins of the state. The natural act of being born in a particular state, being naturalized, or being born of certain parentage confers an irrefutable right of citizenship. While these are generally political rights, they nonetheless reinforce irrevocable conditions that cannot be challenged, no matter how evolving social and economic arrangements distort or magnify

Table 3.1 A Typology of Relative Citizenship: Normative and Instrumental Dimensions

	Political	*Economic*
Normative	David Hart H. G. Frederickson Immanuel Kant Terry Cooper John Rohr John Rawls Michael Walzer	T.H. Marshall Louis Althusser Antonio Gramsci Karl Marx Michel Foucault Jacques Derrida Jürgen Habermas
Instrumental	Aristotle Cicero Hobbes Machiavelli Robert Dahl Francis Fukuyama Hannah Arendt	Plato Max Weber Iris Marion Young

differences and inequalities in society. As socioeconomic status reclassifies society into upper-income, middle-income, and lower-income classes, the US Bill of Rights remains (or ought to remain) a fundamental anchor that equalizes social differences both in the eyes of the law and in the distribution of essential public goods or other economic benefits of citizenship. If we agree that the pursuit of justice is a virtue that any good society should embrace, we also should recognize that as economic inequality disengages individuals from one another, normative citizenship binds and sustains them in the same political estate.

As Brian Cook (1998, p. 226) points out, public administration as a political institution helps to lend a regime its distinctive character. But in carrying out the law, administrative agencies often create, even if by default, particular categories or classes of citizenship and define the proper relations among those classes. In doing so, public administration also shapes behavior, the perceptions that citizens hold of one another and the experiences they have in specific contexts (for instance, between employer and employee). To the extent that "citizen preferences and the continually evolving dynamic of relations among them influence the expression of collective purposes both directly and indirectly through the various avenues available in a democracy" (Cook, 1998, p. 225), "the role of liberal justice, therefore, should be to find principles appropriate for a society in which people disagree fundamentally over many questions, including such metaphysical questions as the nature and character of personal identity" (Gutmann, 1992, p. 126).

Instrumental citizenship, on the other hand, is driven by a person's socioeconomic and political status. It is anchored on an economic and political foundation. Wealth, education, and other perquisites generally associated with upward mobility engender an individual's or group's access to economic and political opportunities that are not generally available to all. It creates unequal possibilities for access to many public and social goods, including the opportunity to participate, directly or indirectly, in processes that shape the nature of political discourse and public policy outcomes. To the extent participation and access are not possible for all, instrumental citizenship creates as well as reinforces social inequalities. While the liberal economic system supports individual effort, private ownership, individual freedom and a free-market system, the inherent contradiction lies in its individualist and reductionist emphasis. As communitarians preach community and group ethic, the liberal system preaches individualism. While the "egalitarian provision of social rights involves an individuation of the population in order to achieve adequate administrative and bureaucratic conditions for social justice, it is the notion of equality of outcome that appears to be incompatible with individualism as the expression of autonomy" (Turner, 1986, p. 121). We may profess equality of citizenship in theory, but in practice it is the inequality of citizenship that we seem to experience. How to reconcile these two contrasting themes is the central dilemma facing contemporary discourse on citizenship.

Of Rights, Obligation, and the Common Good

The idea of rights confers a sense of entitlement as well as responsibility to oneself and others. Because the "idea of rights is nothing other than the idea of virtue introduced into the political world, democratic government brings the idea of political rights down to the lowest citizens, just as the division of property places the idea of right to property in general within the reach of all men" (de Tocqueville, 2000, pp. 93–95). The tendency to view citizenship as an instrumental outcome reinforces the class-based nature of society. While it creates a distinction between "good" and "bad" citizens based on some abstract criteria that may be relevant to the community, the problem is, how does one go about being a good citizen, and when is being a good citizen relevant or rewarding?

Therefore, it is necessary to ask, if citizenship imposes an obligation, what kind of obligation does it impose? There are two possibilities here: normative and political obligation. Normative obligation is a matter of personal choice to learn the difference between what is right and what is wrong—to exercise free will, value judgment, 'love thy neighbor as thyself' (in the Christian admonition), and to safeguard and respect life for its own sake. Political obligation means the external requirements and demands imposed on members of the political community, such as voting, paying taxes, going to work, driving on the right side of the road, obeying traffic conventions, joining the army, and being a good person for the sake of others. Based on the two conceptions of obligation, one could therefore argue that an adequate conception of citizenship must require a balance of rights and responsibilities between individual choice and societal demands within the context of mutual discourse. If moral beliefs depend on supporting social practices for their validity, then we have more reason to believe in a liberal politics of rights than in an Aristotelian politics of the common good (Gutmann, 1992, p. 128). While the Aristotelian method of discovering the "good" by inquiring into the social meaning of roles is of little help in a society where most roles are not attached to a single "good" (Gutmann, 1992, p. 129), an overemphasis on political obligation may mean fewer safeguards for an individual's obligation to one's self.

While "individuals have a responsibility to cooperate with public officials by providing an enabling environment for the execution of the public mandate, they at the same time have a right to equitable representation in the decision making concerning public affairs as well the distribution of incentives and benefits of cooperation" (Kymlicka and Norman, 1994, p. 360). Citizenship as dual obligation should be situated at the intersection where self-interest touches but does not overtake public interest. There must be a renewed emphasis on what the modern state should rightly demand of its citizens, and what citizens should expect from their state. The pursuit of self-interest is not necessarily evil. Even Kant himself thought that "the problem of good government can be solved even for a race of devils" (Galston, 1991, p. 25). He argued that "even if each person pursued his or her own self-interest, without regard for the common good, one set of private interests would check another set of private interests" (Kymlicka and Norman, 1994, p. 359). The real meaning of citizenship demands, first, the affirmation of rights as an irrefutable condition, and second, as reciprocal obligation founded on mutual interest.

Beyond the ontological debate, it has become obvious that the cultural and demographic diversity of the modern state, the dynamism of global trade and Internet communications have almost eliminated the relevance of physical distance in the relationship between societies. Some have even begun to mute the idea of borderless communities and global citizenship. While the orthodox school holds that "effective public administration of the future should be intimately tied to citizenship and to the effectiveness of public managers who work directly with the citizenry" (Frederickson, 1982, p. 501), others argue that citizenship is unattainable in the complex and dynamic structure of contemporary American society (Gawthrop and Waldo, 1984). "To the extent that it is irreversible, the level of complexity—currently evidenced in our society can only be managed but not controlled—hence the future purpose of the craft of administrative management is the revitalization of the character of citizenship and the meaning of citizen" (Gawthrop and Waldo, 1984, p. 103).

There is also the debate as to whether public administrators should behave and operate as administrative entrepreneurs in the market sense of the term (Osborne and Gaebler, 1992), or as administrative conservators (Terry, 1990) of the regime norms and socio-cultural values upon which the United States was built. But the idea of treating public bureaucrats as entrepreneurs, which also suggests that citizens should be treated as customers, is highly problematic. We run the risk of changing the moral and social values on which our constitutional democracy is based. In the conventional sense, while entrepreneurs produce and sell goods and services, customers make choices and bargain with entrepreneurs over how much the goods and services will cost. But if we are talking about publicly provided goods and services, the conferring of rights and privileges, as well as their protection, must take precedence over cost and any perceived entrepreneurial efficiency. "When organizations are appropriated for narrow corporate interests, they effectively impede the broader liberal society from performing essential cultural and political functions" (Stever, 1993, p. 429). The rights and obligations of citizenship equally serve a cultural and political function.

On the Logic of First Principles

In this chapter, I have attempted to reinforce and broaden three sets of arguments: citizenship as a normative right and citizenship as an instrumental outcome; and I also highlighted the dual nature of obligation, and how it is first a matter of choice rather than a response to some external commandment. The thread offered here is that, as a matter of first principle, right confers obligation to oneself more than it confers the right to be obligated to the state. When we demand that citizens be patriotic, are they obligated to do so, or is it a matter of choice? Can we rightfully *force* obligation? In everyday experience, we have our heroes as well as our villains, but when we extol and classify citizenship in terms of what a person does or does not do, citizenship becomes instrumental and thus negates the normative aspect.

In the American liberal state, for instance, we might consider two methods of recruitment into the armed forces. One is the volunteer system (by choice) and the other is the draft (by mandate). But experience informs us that in a situation in which one refuses to answer to the draft or flees to another country thus running from an obligation to the state, the person essentially loses the fabric (self-regard) of what it means to be a citizen. We normally explain this behavior as being unpatriotic, selfish and amoral. While this type of attitude is not suggested here, nor should it necessarily be condoned, it should be recognized only as an affirmation of right rather than a denial of citizenship. In the very difficult process of balancing fundamental rights with self-interest and obligation to the community, the concept of rights should be set apart as a moral category. In the normative sense of the term, the draft dodger is a tragic hero: Though his behavior may invoke the free-rider problem, he nonetheless remains a citizen with no less entitlement than all other citizens who chose otherwise. Even when we deny him the right to vote, that in itself ought not be construed as an impediment to his citizenship but as a punitive sanction meant to deter as well as affirm an acceptable social convention.

The same principle should apply to people who are not able to pay their taxes, either because they are poor or because there are other incumbent priorities that deny them the opportunity to pay their debts to society. Though they make no instrumental contribution to the welfare of society, and though their inability to pay seems to protect their self-interest more than the public good, they are still citizens to the best of that definition. Given the choice, "individuals are thus in both accounts primary and society secondary, and the identification of individual interests is prior to and independent of the construction of any moral or social bonds between them" (MacIntyre, 1992, p. 58). As Emile Durkheim suggests, all aspects of social phenomena and life tend toward an independent existence: "While laws are embodied in codes; the currents of daily life are recorded in statistical figures and historical monuments; fashions are preserved in costumes; and taste in works of art" (Durkheim, 1994, p. 440).

Conversely, if we take Aristotle's contention that a person's citizenship is manifested through political participation and working for the good of the *polis* (the state), then citizenship can be affirmed to the extent that one does something to advance the general interest of the *polis*. While this reinforces the class-based nature of society, it also conceives of citizenship as a means to an end rather than as an end in itself. Though this seems to be the dominant theme in the contemporary literature and discourse on citizenship, I argue that the above conceptualization negates the normative aspect of citizenship, which should remain irrefutable. As a society, we must seek to revitalize the civic equalitarian precepts that are implicit in the liberal tradition, but which are fading in our time. Experience confirms that in circumstances in which our administrative practices have not been known to correspond to our constitutional foundations, inequality prevails and our sense of communal citizenship dissipates. It will require the role of legislators to reinforce the laws or even making new ones where necessary and the action of public bureaucrats as both moral and cultural agents of change and citizenship.

For the simple fact that inequalities in socioeconomic status also engender inequalities in access to political and economic opportunities, we must rely on our legislators and bureaucrats as 'defenders of the faithful' to transform our society and its institutions in pursuit of the normative ethos. This can be done only if they aspire to bear objective witness to the sanctity of the equal protection clause in the application of the law and the due process provisions of the Fifth and Fourteenth amendments, respectively, as well as the horizontal privileges and immunities granted in Article IV of the US Constitution. From a "perspective that takes into account the essential nature of political institutions—that they are both instrumental to and constitutive of the regime—the normative implications are particularly deep and far-reaching for the theory and practice of public management" (Cook, 1998, p.227).

The issue of access to health care has remained a Herculean task to reconcile among our public policy makers. Should we have a universal health insurance (as a right of citizenship), or should we resort to the instrumental opportunities provided by the market system? Today, about 40 million Americans do not have health insurance, and if we add those who may be in a transitional state, the figure may reach 60 million at any point in time. The irony is that if we rely on everyone obtaining insurance coverage through his or her employment or paying out of pocket, this possibility can hardly come true. Alternatively, if we abandon those who cannot pay to their own fate, then the demand on indigent care will continue to increase dramatically, at a greater cost to society. While it might be permissible to state here that policy controversies signify disputes among institutional actors who sponsor conflicting frames, seemingly intractable policy controversies, such as we have in the American health care system, can be bridged by refocusing policy priorities to serve the normative imperative as a matter of first principle grounded in an irrefutable right of citizenship.

The Incommensurability of Democratic Liberalism

The democratic ethos reinforces individual freedom but at the same time advocates pluralist participation in public discussion and political decision making. Democracy has a constitutive quality that embraces a lot of things. It is a state of mind, a method of governance, an ideology, a discourse and a mechanism of engagement both in elections and in decision making. "Beyond the electoral system itself, democracy requires rights and freedoms, if only because individuals need the space that these provide in order to discover or develop their preferences" (Dowding, 2004, p.26). But it also requires "vital dialogue that includes elements of empirical investigation, interpretation, critique, narrative, conflict and conflict resolution" (Caspary, 2000, p.9). Hence, the ideal discursive space is one that involves political contestation consisting of elements of agreement and disagreement so that in the end they "would lead to the discovery of common interests, not simply bargaining over private interests" (Caspary, 2000, p.9).

For John Dewey, "democracy involves the breaking down of barriers of class, race, and national territory which keeps men from perceiving the full import of their activity" (Caspary, 2000, p. 14); hence, and to the extent that democracy fosters vigorous interchange of ideas and perspectives, people would, indeed, be influenced by one another (Capsary, 2000, p. 14). Democracy therefore, "is about people's right to participate, and the *terms* of their participation, in the discourse leading to the formation of social values that inform political choices that manifest themselves in public policies and actions" (Franck, 1999, p. 262). But beyond rhetorical flourish, democracy, in actuality, is less about people's right to participate than the terms of their participation. In the absence of direct democracy, which in all probabilities would be quite untenable in every situation and at all times, the terms by which people participate in the democratic enterprise is through their vote.

But in matters of policy making or deciding crucial choices about government priorities, the people participate only indirectly through their elected representatives. As is most evident, even though they may harbor the interest of the electorate, legislators or representatives have interests of their own, set apart from the interests of those who elected them. The choices and programs they support are, more often than not, influenced by their own self-interests and prospects for re-election, even when those choices may be inimical to those of their constituencies. Ironically, while the legitimacy of public policies in liberal states derives from the policies' assumed *representativeness*, it remains unclear in what manner and under what circumstances we are able to agree whether the character of this *representativeness* applies equally, or rather fairly, to each and every citizen.

The Liberal Agency and the Constitution of Rights

The liberal conception of citizenship is that of individual "allegiance to the state as something that enforces the rule of law and acts as a protector of universal human rights" (Beiner, 2003, p. 167) in the distribution of public goods and equal access to political opportunities. There is a paradoxical relationship between the rule of law and the autonomous individual minding his own business and opting to be left alone. But the free exercise of autonomy is problematic in the liberal democratic state where the law sets the boundaries of such autonomy *apriori* and where pursuit of the common good might collide (as it often does) with an untrammeled expression of individual autonomy. The liberal state seeks to offer it all, but the reality of the human condition is that, sooner or later, unhindered autonomy, choice and freedom, lead to conditions where individuals will most likely run afoul of the law. Liberal democracies are supposed to provide for individual rights but are at the same time obligated to safeguard those rights in the public interest. "Citizenship in this context, is the right to or not vote, to be left alone, not to be assaulted by the state, or incriminated by one's own statements" (Raskin, 2004, p. 21).

The liberal argument that a conflict of rights that undermines a provision in the Bill of Rights must be weighed in favor of that provision creates a paradox because the conflict must be adjudicated in light of the fact that most civic rights are not limited to the private sphere but are also in the public sphere where other expressions of rights are in competition. But those who subscribe to the liberal political virtue counter this on the premise that while "other citizens may be reasonable people who are worthy of respect, good citizens are willing to acknowledge there may be differences between them and others about conceptions of the good" (Soutphommasane, 2012, p. 109). Hence, provided that citizens are committed to liberal political justice, disagreements based on divergence in social values or philosophical beliefs are immaterial (Soutphommasane, 2012, p. 109). But how do we know *apriori* that other people will recognize these differences, and what about those citizens who do not subscribed to the tenets of liberal political justice? Although assumptions may serve a purpose in reducing the odds of making a bad decision, their ability to transcend reality can only be based on probabilities.

Even the liberal normative emphasis on philosophical neutrality—*neutrality in aim* and *neutrality in effect*—may be untenable, simply because one can only be neutral in an issue in which one does not have a stake whatsoever. Citizens in liberal democracies have a collective interest in seeing to the survival of the democratic project, but then collective interest is a summation of individual interests. In the sense that philosophical or ethical values are nothing but products of reflection on the situation or the issue at hand, John Dewey argues that reflection, psychologically speaking, is not always impartial; and "quite often, reflection is a mere rationalization of self-interest or a point of view taken in advance" (Somjee, 1968, p. 38).

The Dworkinian meaning of neutrality in the sense that "the state is not to do anything intended to favor or promote any particular comprehensive doctrine rather than another" (Beiner, 2003, p. 55) does not effectively advance the liberal argument and the quest for the common good. We can take for instance the debate on health care coverage in the United States. There are those who favor universal insurance of the type they have in Canada or in some of the Scandinavian countries, but there are others who favor maintenance of the market system and the private sector provided fee-for-service payment regime. The differences in this debate have generally been along ideological lines, with liberals going for the former and conservatives, for the most part, going for the latter.

Various government administrations have tried and failed and in several measures only settled for a less than ideal solution to the problem of rising health care coverage and medical access in the United States. Ironically, if we follow Ronald Dworkin's neutrality thesis as above, neither the idea of universal health insurance nor the private sector market system would offer a sufficient solution, since the adoption of any one of them would essentially mean the negation of the other. Hence, Dworkin's approach "seems peculiarly insufficient for providing satisfactory responses to many of the inequalities that do characterize contemporary societies, other than by presenting them as the product of autonomous choices" (Armstrong, 2006, p. 58). When individuals, for one reason or the other, do not have health insurance coverage and the need for it becomes ever more present, individual autonomy ends once the state steps in to provide the needed assistance in the form of Medicare or Medicaid or universal health insurance if that were available.

Yet, liberals have mostly been the ones at the forefront of the debate for universal health coverage in the United States. While the emphasis is on equality of access and opportunity, the liberal idea of equality is premised on the fact that "government should show equal concern for all individuals, and should respect their integrity and dignity as individuals; but they do not mean, by this, that everyone should all be treated the same way all of the time" (Armstrong, 2006, p. 59). Instead, they mean "treating individuals on the basis of what is distinctively individual about them—and this may require treating different individuals differently" (Armstrong, 2006, p. 59). This is the same view held by Iris Marion Young in her "differentiated citizenship" and Will Kymlicka in his "multicultural citizenship," both of which call for special and exclusionary provisions for groups that fall into their categories. But how we achieve a semblance of citizenship-as-community and as a collective norm in light of these competing narratives raises a corresponding question regarding the liberal emphasis on the self-interest and autonomy of the individual and the common good of the public.

The idea of popular sovereignty has also come under further scrutiny. While citizens can join associational groupings of their own choice and ideological persuasions, or make independent decisions regarding whether to participate, the idea of sovereignty also draws on the role of autonomy in making publicly relevant choices, such as whether to vote or not in an election. E.S. Morgan (1988) argues that the claim of popular sovereignty—taken to imply that people as a whole do engage or ever have engaged in extensive public deliberation on an egalitarian basis in order to resolve directly any concrete issues of public life, is a myth or fiction. The reason is that it would be impossible for most people because of differences in the existing social stratification as well as relative differences in other aspects of political and economic life.

Effective deliberation requires that people have access to similar types of information or, at least, have a minimal stake in the object of deliberation. Other demanding requirements of industrial society and the welfare state make this possible only for some, at different times and under different conditions. The exercise of popular sovereignty in the substantive sense of the term is not possible where interests and conditions for participation are relative and conditional. As pointed out by Rogers Smith (1997, p. 36), "political decision making is in reality almost always more a matter of elite bargaining than popular deliberation; and in so far as there is such deliberation, most people do not participate in it." And those that do participate, often differ greatly in their resources, and it rarely determines actual policy outcomes" (Smith, 1997, p. 36). But we also make the mistake of construing the idea of participation as having an intrinsic value of its own when, in fact, it is simply a process of civic involvement or engagement. The value of participation lies only in the valence or utility of that for which public participation is necessary or required. More often than not, public participation end up not yielding much except that it helps to legitimize a central democratic norm of popular involvement in decision making and governance.

Public Interest and Self-Interest

It is always assumed that there is a public interest that serves the interest of everyone and to which everyone ascribes. While there may be several occasions where this would be the case, in the greater majority of cases, people rarely agree on what the public interest should be and how it serves their own particular aspirations or interests. In fact, democratic discourse encourages this disagreement, and much of what is done in the US Congress, for example, is focused on deliberations aimed at achieving a consensus that reflects an assumed public interest based on which logic attracts the most votes. Even at that, members of Congress still do not succeed in securing a true public interest for the simple reason that some legislators may have voted for an alternative option but were defeated because there were more votes on the other side. Their dignified resignation to the outcome does not *ipso facto* imply a willing acceptance of the majority choice as representing the public interest; it is based on a technical issue rather than the absence of any other acceptable means of conflict resolution in the democratic discourse.

Hence, the idea of a public interest is a presumptive construct—superimposing any credible disagreement on the subject matter by recourse to a de facto consensus premised on majority rule. Majority rule is therefore a simple way of seeking the elusive public interest, not by any semblance of unanimous consent, but by engaging in mathematical reductionism or a game of numbers. It points to the fact that "in shaping the doctrine of the public interest in a pluralist context, quantity becomes the benchmark of quality, and that which is desired is readily seen as that which is desirable" (Gawthrop and Waldo, 1984, p. 105). Although the notion of public interest has been a central theme that continues to resonate in the mainstream of democratic idealism, but in the "objective world of practical, pragmatic politics, it is purely a mechanistic contrivance designed to justify the outcomes of balance of power coalition building and decision making" (Gawthrop and Waldo, 1984, p. 105).

Alternatively, self-interest is a generally inescapable aspect of human nature both in individual matters and in matters of the general public. Even when we encourage public officials or bureaucrats to supplant their self-interest with the public interest, and if and when they comply they are still serving their self-interest no less than before they were asked to seek the public interest. This is so because by complying to serve the *public interest*, they are also serving their own *self-interest* in the sense that they get to keep their jobs by doing what they were told to do. I have argued elsewhere (See Kalu, 2003b, p. 556) that as every ordinary individual, bureaucrats are rational actors driven by self-interest. The simple idea of a willingness to live and to be able to support one's family is a function of self-interest, and it is to serve this primary end that most individuals seek public service or other forms of employment. If public servants were not paid for their work, very few would go into public service simply for altruistic reasons. Remove the compensatory incentive and you will quickly find out that many of them would shirk any moral responsibility to the public interest but would instead opt for their own self-preservation.

Every urge to act in the public interest is filtered through the lens of self-interest, because the sense of accomplishment and the ennobled self-regard and collective appreciation it may induce are equally matters of self-interest. People often say: I *feel* comfortable doing that; it matters very much to *me* or helping out that way was very important to *me*. And although their actions may have served the public interest, they acted only because they felt *comfortable* about it or that it mattered to *them* so much. Without these self-interest-laden filters, they may likely not have acted in the first place. For Hobbes, "human beings are moved by desires and aversions which generate a state of perpetual restlessness; and seeking always 'more intense delight', they are profoundly self-interested" (Held, 1989, p. 15). Hence, it is in the pursuit of power and self-interest that defines the human condition.

Justice as Relativity: Categories with a Difference

The moral basis of *justice* has gone through various conceptualizations; it would be appropriate to ask a simple question—*whose* justice? There are variations of justice as fairness, as virtue, as lawfulness, as due process or as giving each person his or her due. The last part thus also invokes the idea of positive or negative justice, which also begs the question as to *which* justice would be applicable in specific situations and occurrences. Part of the reason people disagree so often about justice, particularly among liberal societies, is that we assess it based on what it results in (the outcome) as opposed to what it stands for. For those on the losing end, it would not be justice but injustice; for those on the winning side, it would certainly be justice. As Aristotle (1985, p. 1135a10) points out in the *Nicomachean Ethics*—"an act of injustice is different from what is unjust, and an act of justice from what is just." It is often difficult to separate the dual nature of justice (its substantive and procedural qualities) from each other since, in most cases, both qualities could be applicable under the same circumstance. Yet, if we accept the fact that justice stands for distinguishing the difference between right and wrong and applying reward or sanctions accordingly (in terms of what Aristotle calls *rectificatory justice*), then we must also have a common agreement concerning those things that ought to be construed as right or wrong. In the more realistic absence of that, justice is therefore reduced to its *relativeness* depending on which side of the divide the bone of contention weighs more heavily.

In *The Republic*, Plato depicts a scene in which Glaucon and Socrates were engaged in dialogue concerning the meaning of justice. The account offered deviates from any consideration of moral equivalency but is founded on the illustration that when each of the three classes (businessmen, auxiliaries and guardians) perform the social duties consistent with their natural qualities, and if in the end this arrangement contributes to the excellence of the city (state), then this can be construed as justice. Justice therefore is embodied in a man's inward self, concern and interest in seeing that a harmonious whole is achieved when each and every one performs and minds his own business without intervening in that of others. Hence, justice is produced by establishing in the mind a similar natural relation of control and subordination among its constituent parts (Plato, 1955, p. 154).

Justice in this regard is a matter of the proper arrangement of social and political functions in the city in such a way that everyone is assigned to responsibilities for which his or her nature (or natural gifts) permits. Anything to the contrary would be injustice and thus would be harmful to the welfare of the city.

For Aristotle, the value of justice is premised in its distributive quality as well as in its expression and effect on the *other*. Justice therefore is a form of complete virtue in relation to another. It is the virtue that the just person expresses in just actions and decisions. But justice is also a matter of giving each person his due in the sense that "equality for the people involved in an enterprise will be the same as for the things involved; since the relation between the people will be the same as the relation between the things involved" (Aristotle, 1985, p. 123). But when the people involved are not equals they should receive unequal shares, because justice demands that equals receive equal shares and unequals receive unequal shares. In this regard, proportional equality would be consistent with the aim of justice. But above all, Aristotle considers justice as a teleological movement toward the mean; because it concerns an intermediate condition, while injustice concerns the extremes (Aristotle, 1985, p. 134). But since it would be difficult to know when an individual act has reached or crossed the mean, the contention is that the most just of individual acts would be those guided by *temperance* or the 'principle of the golden mean'—a mid-range between two extremes.

From the liberal point of view, the key tenets of justice should be expected to satisfy a set of basic assumptions premised on the concept of rights, equality and the application of the rule of law in such a way that it is the same, particularly in all cases that are similar. One of the major purveyors of liberal justice is John Rawls, whose conception of justice takes as its starting point the argument that "the most reasonable principles of justice are those that everyone would accept and agree to from a fair position"—a fair position in this regard being that of "a rational agent situated behind a veil of ignorance" (Rawls, 1971, p. 136) such that he does not know what place in society he will occupy. From the vantage point of being in the *original position* of equality, such a person would be indifferent and would have no prior knowledge of his class or position in life, would be unaware of any risk involved or benefits that may derive from making particular choices concerning any distribution of goods in the social order. "They do not know how the various alternatives will affect their own particular case and they are obliged to evaluate principles solely on the basis of general considerations" (Rawls, 1971, pp. 136–137). Such a distribution must meet the standard of two principles of justice, viz (Rawls, 1971, p. 302):

- First principle—Each person is to have an equal right to the most extensive total system of equal basic liberties compatible with a similar system of liberty for all, and
- Second principle—Social and economic inequalities are to be arranged so that they are both (a) to the greatest benefit to the least advantaged, consistent with the just savings principle, and (b) attached to offices and positions open to all under conditions of fair equality of opportunity.

For Rawls, justice requires that all "social primary goods—liberty and opportunity, income and wealth and the bases of self-respect—are to be distributed equally unless an unequal distribution of any or all of these goods is to the advantage of the least favored" (Rawls, 1971, p. 303). Rawls's "theory is concerned with the basic structure of society, and the way it allocates rights, duties, wealth, power and opportunities; but underlying the 'veil of ignorance' is a moral argument whose main idea is that the distribution of income and opportunity should not be based on factors that are *arbitrary*" (Sandel, 2009, pp. 152–153). It is also premised on the fact that "we must somehow nullify the effects of specific contingencies which put men at odds and tempt them to exploit social and natural circumstances to their own advantage" (Sandel, 2007, p. 219). Hence, "liberty in adopting a conception of the good (or fairness) is limited only by principles that are deduced from a doctrine which imposes no prior constraints on these conceptions" (Sandel, 1982, p. 60). In a fair distribution of social goods, although Rawls grants primacy to justice over efficiency, one can equally argue that the two terms are inseparable since they reinforce each other; because a distribution that is fairly done could also be construed as having been done efficiently hence would be considered just as long as each person got his or her fair share and is satisfied by it.

Many critiques of the Rawlsian concept of the 'veil of ignorance' (Nozick, 1974; Sandel, 1982, 2007, 2009) point out that a *rational* agent would not necessarily be expected to operate from behind a veil from which he knows nothing about the issue he is dealing with. On the other hand, Rawls's conception of the principle of equality based on needs, particularly of the 'worst off' sector of the community in respect to income, wealth or other goods, as well as the efficacy of the 'difference principle' in all situations, seems inconsistent with the free-market ideals of the liberal capitalist economy. While the free-market economy is premised on the competitive spirit and effort of individuals and businesses, free choice with respect to market entry and exit and the role of the invisible hand in the regulation of supply and demand, Rawls's argument would need a proactive government intervention instead of the market to redistribute basic social and economic goods.

Since the market alone may not be able to provide a fair distribution to the fullest extent and degree that Rawls would prefer, in what areas and to what extent should the political action of government be used to justify moral arbitrariness? Perhaps, this would be applicable where existing opportunities are unequal or where initial starting points in life are skewed in favor of one and not the other. But then this still begs the question as to whether an individual's adverse economic situation, for which the cause may be unknown or could be traced directly to the individual himself, could also evoke specific moral questions and responsibility placed on others or the public. Are all economic and social inequalities a result of someone's moral deficiency thereby raising issues of culpability and restitution?

In all, there should be a general understanding that justice cannot construct or create its own meaning; rather justice derives from the cultivation of the soul in such a way that every thought or action is directed to some good. For the simple fact that any "idea of justice supposes a *rule of conduct* and a *sentiment* which ought to sanction the rule" (Mill, 2007, p. 41), justice requires the exercise of *moral identity* and *moral obligation* in dealing with matters within the private or public spheres. "Moral identity has to do with how people understand themselves as moral, such as when a person who considers himself truthful always feels the pressure to engage in truth-saying as a way of validating his self-concept" (Clair, 2015, p. 165); and as a result, "moral identity functions as a self-regulatory mechanism that motivates moral action" (Aquino and Reed, 2002; Damon and Hart, 1992).

In my own view, the most thorough explication of the idea of moral obligation is the account provided by Panaetius as illustrated by Cicero in *On Duties* III. By answering three basic questions (Cicero, 1960, p. 161), Panaetius argues that an individual should be able to make a choice or judgment that points to the right and just action:

- Is a thing morally right or wrong?
- Is it advantageous or disadvantageous?
- If apparent right and apparent advantage clash, what is to be the basis for our choice between them?

Of the three questions, the third might seem to be the most difficult to answer, since according to some people, "advantage can never conflict with right, for the fact that everything which is morally right is advantageous, and there can be no advantage in anything which is not right" (Cicero, 1960, pp. 162–163). But I argue that it is conceivable for right to be in conflict with advantage—*in the distribution of the advantage*. The question that ought to be asked is: Who benefits most from the advantage, and who benefits least? At whose expense was the advantage achieved, and at what cost? In this regard, right can certainly conflict with advantage when the advantage is at the expense of others. Rawls would certainly argue that such a right does not make sense if the advantage was obtained at the expense of the least advantaged in society; and Aristotle would equally raise the concern as to whose well-being the *advantage* serves—that of the individual or the *polis*?

The Case against Majority Rule

> *It is of the very essence of democratic governments that the empire of the majority be absolute in them; for outside of the majority, in democracies, there is nothing which resists.*
>
> (Alexis de Tocqueville, 2000, p. 102)

Justice as virtue, fairness or due process is indivisible, and its meaning cannot be rightfully adjudicated by recourse to mathematical numbers. That in itself would be a negation such that in the search for justice we end up undermining it. In liberal democracies, the most pluralistic basis for making political choices and decisions is the principle of majority rule. As a mechanism for choice making, it does not necessarily yield conclusions based on the best logic or facts; rather, it seeks the determination of specific choices by relying on the largest number, which may, in fact, have little or no bearing on the substance and accuracy of reasoning behind the facts. The concept of majority rule does not offer the ideal choice for making most political decisions; hence, the question arises whether it can justly be used for all choice arbitration in democratic politics. For instance, in a multiethnic society, majority rule has a curious way of making democracy undemocratic. As illustrated in Kalu (2008, p. 188), if one of the major ethnic groups has a majority, then it would be able to dominate the government (especially the legislature) on an almost permanent basis as long as it does not allow its votes to split among two or more parties. Majority interests would, more often than not, trump minority or collective interests.

In his rather loose defense of majority rule, Rawls argues that "the fundamental criterion for judging any procedure is the justice of its likely outcome" (1971, p. 230), hence "if the various sectors of society have reasonable confidence in one another and share a common conception of justice, the rule by bare majorities may succeed fairly well" (Rawls, 1971, p. 231). But where this "underlying agreement is lacking, the majority principle becomes more difficult to justify" (Rawls, 1971, p. 231). The above Rawlsian pseudo-justification is too "thin" and does not provide sufficient grounding for the majority rule principle and therefore should be rejected for the following reasons.

First, we may not be able to know the *likely* justice of the outcome *apriorily* until the outcome has occurred, and by then it may already be too late. Second, for the simple reason that liberal democracies encourage diversity and difference of opinions, the various sectors of society Rawls talks about may not have reasonable confidence in one another or share the same conception of justice all of the time. In fact, the *raison d'etre* of democratic liberal states is the opportunity to differ and have competing ideas about government and society. The mere fact that "different persons are situated differently will assure that some differences of power and knowledge persist, allowing agreements, even voluntary ones, to be influenced by factors arbitrary from a moral point of view" (Sandel, 1998, p. 114). Third, even if all members of society share the same views about justice (and they rarely do), the sharing of similar views has no bearing on what the outcome of justice would be. In fact, any abridgement of justice would become even more noticeable in circumstances in which all members of society share a similar point of view regarding its scope and meaning.

But the use of the principle of majority rule to adjudicate specific political or moral questions may end up reinforcing not justice for all, but injustice for some. Numbers alone do not in the absolute sense justify a superiority of logic and reason, nor does it constitute a demonstration of truth or evidence of reality for choosing one option over another. Taken collectively, a majority is simply a group of individuals who have opinions and most often interests contrary to other individuals whom one calls the minority (de Tocqueville, 2000, p. 106). But does that in any way suggest that the majority has a command on knowledge and virtue rather than the minority?

While lamenting the inauspicious role of majority rule in American democracy, the French jurist Alexis de Tocqueville (2000, pp. 103–104) points out that its moral claim is based essentially "on the idea that there is more enlightenment and wisdom in many men who are brought together than in one alone, more enlightenment and wisdom in the number than in the choice of legislators; hence the interest of the greatest number must be preferred to those of the minority." But in doing so, we end up enshrining a practice that, more often than not, leads to abuse of power thereby undermining the very tradition of representative democracy. This is evidenced by the fact that "once a majority has formed on a question, there are virtually no obstacles which can stop, or even slow down its march and allow it the time to listen to the complaints of those it crushes in passing; and the consequences of this are disastrous and dangerous for the future" (de Tocqueville, 2000, p. 104). "Liberty thus, is in danger when this power finds no obstacle before it which can check its march and give it the time to moderate itself on its own" (de Tocqueville, 2000, p. 108).

We can take two instances in American politics where the principle of majority rule only ended up making a lot of people angry and frustrated, even as they accepted their fate with resigned indignation. The Electoral College vote is a procedural mechanism for electing the President of the United States. In a winner-take-all contest, the winner of the majority of the popular vote in each state takes all of the Electoral College votes for that state, even when the winning candidate has a percentage or two more than the candidate that lost. How fair is it that after all the campaigns and expenditure of effort, time, and money, yet one does not secure a single Electoral College vote even when the losing candidate got 49% of the vote? In many states that have millions of voters, the support of 49% translates to a lot of people for which the candidate receives no reward. The irony is that there is no way, even remotely, to determine whether the 51% that voted for the winning candidate understood the issues or are more intuitively knowledgeable than the 49% that voted for the other candidate. And this also applies to the winning candidate, even though the criterion for the winner-take-all is premised on the majority vote.

We can also look at the nature of voting in the United States Senate where out of 100 members, a 51/49 vote would grant judgment to the policy preference or point of view of the 51. Beside the fact that 49 out of 100 is a lot of people with equally important opinions and ideas, in a representative democracy, do the opinions and policy preferences of the 49 Senators matter? If so, to what extent can these equally be accommodated to the logic of majority rule? How do we know that the majority (51) is right and the minority (49) wrong? It can be argued that a minority or even a single Senator can hold up a debate (filibuster) on the Senate floor on an issue that he or she does not support, but this tactic is rarely used and is often considered a nuisance factor that can be ended by invoking a cloture or 60 votes (a majority) of members of the Senate. How does this method reflect the interest of justice as due process?

Although "justice is ordinarily regarded as an attribute of outcomes, whereas democracy is ordinarily regarded as an attribute of process; it can be the case that a seemingly impartial process often yields an outcome that is itself partial, giving everything to one part of the community and nothing to others" (Goodin, 2004, p. 98). And this point is equally reinforced by Keith Dowding (2004, p. 25) to the effect that "democratic procedures and just social outcomes are not the same thing." He argues that given the "competitive nature of democracy and the fact that most, if not all, political issues concern the distribution of scarce resources, unjust distributions (under the same theory of justice) are likely to be the norm rather than the exception" (Dowding, 2004, p. 25). As in "the case of majority tyranny over the minority, and invariably so, majority rule is no less democratic for its being tyrannical; it is simply less just" (Gooding, 2000, p. 98).

In his *Dilemmas of Pluralist Democracy*, Robert Dahl also proffers a cautionary note stating that, "if a body of citizens were to deprive any citizen of any fundamental right necessary to the democratic process, then by its own action it would violate the criteria of the democratic process" (Dahl, 1982, p. 49). Therefore, and if we accept the unvarnished premise that "the function of the political realm is to render service to individual interests and purposes, to protect citizens in the exercise of their rights, and to leave them unhindered in the pursuit of whatever individual and collective interests and purposes they might have" (Oldfield, 1998, p. 76), it is debatable and even contestable that the majority rule principle can be used as a feasible platform to validate and secure the full extent of these rights and interests.

Similarly, we are also confronted with the *utilitarian* argument in favor of the *greatest good of the greatest number* which, in itself, implies the aggregation of utility. But how do we accurately and without conjecture, measure every *good*, particularly those that could fall under the category of relative pleasure, benefit, leisure, comfort and the like? By what other criteria do we establish the *greatest* good, other than by using numbers (more people) in this regard? Do numbers alone confer entitlement to a *good,* and what is the qualitative or normative relationship between a number (a numeric value) and a specific good? To what extent do mere numbers alone justify any moral compass used in the distribution or redistribution of specific public goods? For John Dewey, answers to these questions are a forgone conclusion because "institutional design is always partial, contestable, and experimental" (Caspary, 2000, p. 14). This problem is more magnified in the sense that most "egalitarian debates are largely about what is to be equalized and maximized—utility, welfare, resources, opportunities, capabilities, and power—but all too often say little about the institutions which are to deliver the goods" (Dowding, 2004, p. 29).

The point remains that the "greatest good of the greatest number" is only possible if it leaves a victim in its wake, that is, by creating a *lesser* good for the *lesser* number. While impartiality is a necessary condition of both democracy and justice, it is not a sufficient condition (Goodin, 2004, p. 99). The demands are much higher, and majority rule has been used to unnecessarily simplify it. But to grant more benefits and opportunity to "some people for no more reason than that they have more votes is ordinarily substantively unjust" (Goodin, 2004, p. 98). "Arguments for principles of justice are supposed to deliver the institutions that are thought to follow from those principles; socially just institutions must also take into account the incentives they create for people in order to shape a society in accord with their justificatory principles" (Dowding, 2004, pp. 29–30).

As forms of decision making and choice, the principles of majority rule and utilitarianism are economic means of resolving social and political issues for which people disagree or for which alternative methods of distribution or conflict resolution may be difficult to find. While both approaches normally end up simplifying what, in fact, are hard choices, "economy should never be used as justification for actions which threaten the common good; and neither should the application of the 'greatest good of the greatest number' be allowed to jeopardize the constitutional guarantees of a minority" (Cooper, 1984, p. 148). "For this reason justice denies that the loss of freedom for some is made right by a greater good shared by others" (Rawls, 2007, p. 203). To the same effect, de Tocqueville argues that the seeming "omnipotence of the majority, and the rapid and absolute manner in which its desires are complied with in the United States, not only makes the law unstable, it also exercises the same influence on the execution of the law and on the action of public administration" (2000, p. 105).

Ironically, pluralist liberal democracies are supposed to entertain multiple and even divergent opinions on critical issues of public governance, but of what use will it be if the views of some become public policy while those of the few are of no accord? Of what use is the ideal of citizen engagement in public deliberation if at the end of the day, the vote of the many will trump the views of the few? It is on this very premise that "when a nation is divided between several great irreconcilable interests, the right of the majority is often refused acceptance because it becomes too difficult to submit to it" (de Tocqueville, 2000, p. 104). Using the principle of majority rule to end further debate on a critical issue is very shortsighted for two main reasons. First, it is possible that continuous deliberation on an issue could yield better ideas and solutions based on individual intuitive abilities without being subjected to a vote count; second, there may not be any empirical referent to suggest that majorities are always right. There is no empirical correlation between majority vote and the correctness of a choice. In the likely situation where such may seem to be the case, the outcome could be the result of random coincidences that neither the majority nor the minority could have controlled.

Due Process and the Etiology of Rights

The idea of due process implies that people should be treated the same way when they qualify under the same or similar conditions. In the end, due process is a means of validating specific rights but is also a means of securing equal treatment and, invariably, justice. In addition to rule by precedent, judicial rulings in the United States are supposed to follow and secure due process for all. The right to due process is granted in the Fifth and Fourteenth Amendments of the US Constitution. There are two types of due process: Procedural due process grants procedural rights and justice. It seeks to answer a basic question: Was he treated in the same way as the other person, both of whom qualify for similar treatment under similar cases as applicable? The same rights, the same benefits and privileges and the same procedures of treatment that are applied to one must be applied to all under similar conditions. Substantive due process "holds that government is barred from enforcing policies that are irrational, unfair, unreasonable, or unjust, even if such policies do not run counter to other specific constitutional prohibitions" (Otis et al., 2015, p. 25). One also might ask the question whether one is able under the law to secure similar 'quantity' of remedies sought in a case or whether one's share of benefits is seen as being fair and equitable. However, because of the overwhelmingly qualitative nature of due process, there may be situations in which it may not be able to secure justice for all in the absolute sense of the term. While some might claim that due process has been served, others might claim otherwise. And so, whose due process and whose justice can we claim to have been served in this regard? Because we rely on the courts to adjudicate issues of this nature, judicial opinions will be required to make determinations on a case-by-case basis. How and with what criteria is this determination made?

"One function of the Supreme Court is to keep peace between rival social groups adhering to rival and incompatible principles of justice by displaying a fairness which consists in even-handedness in its adjudication" (MacIntyre, 1992, p. 62). But how much fairness or even-handedness is displayed when the Supreme Court bases its judicial rulings on the majority vote of the Justices? There are nine Justices in the Supreme Court, and five votes constitute a majority and four the minority. By this, due process and justice itself become reduced to numbers irrespective of the persuasiveness or superiority of the argument of the minority. When they use the principle of majority rule to make legal determinations, it is less of a judicial affirmation than a political judgment.

When they disagree on an issue, how are we to know with absolute certainty that the opinion of the majority has more substantive legal merit than that of the minority? When the nine Justices review an issue in the context of the same legal or constitutional provision but come up with different interpretations and/or views, it could be about inherent contradictions within such constitutional provision as opposed to a lack of intuitive logic on the part of the Justices themselves. The "judgement about who is entitled to receive what service, who is to be accorded what treatment, or who is to be taxed at what rate creates legal categories that singles out this or that group for attention" (Ducat, 2013, p. 1142). Therefore, relying on the applicability of majority rule in the resolution of intractable judicial questions is a rather superficial way of resolving the differences within and between legal categories. We are not sure which side is correct except by recourse to a numeric vote that may have little to do with the actual substance of the case; judicial majority rule grants neither due process nor justice for all, and "as such, legal categories necessarily discriminate" (Ducat, 2013, p. 1142).

In the June 26, 2015, ruling on *Obergefell v. Hodges*, the Justices in a 5–4 decision ruled in favor of same-sex marriage, by implication determining such restriction as unconstitutional. Writing the majority judicial opinion in this case, Justice Anthony Kennedy invoked the due process and equal protection clauses of the Fourteenth Amendment. In the end, there was no unanimity on the part of the Justices, but the way they could resolve the deadlock was not based on the superiority or correctness of the arguments from each side. They had to resort to a political mechanism as opposed to using judicial logic. They had to vote, and the resolution of the court was made by majority rule. For the fact that there is only one US Constitution, *due process* also demands that the Justices have the same understanding of *due process* as well as justice. If and when they disagree as to the meaning and the constitutional interpretation, then they are bound not to offer different judgments and adjudication in matters for which only the principle of *unanimity* can be said to secure justice and due process.

This point can be drawn more succinctly from Thomas Hobbes's argument in the *Leviathan*: "When question is of the meaning of written laws, he is not the interpreter of them that writeth a commentary upon them; for commentaries are commonly more subject to cavil than the text, hence need other commentaries—and in this process, there will be no end of such interpretation" (1994, p. 182). The only way the Justices could get out of the dilemma was to apply the majority vote, so the issue may still be unresolved since no side can claim that the logic of its argument was superior to that of the other. Because a mere majority vote cannot decide that, the ruling can be seen as a political judgment in which ideology and judicial activism played more central roles than the logic and substance of the arguments. But then what type of due process and justice does the Fourteenth Amendment grant, and to whom in this regard? In addition to the *due process* provision, the equality (equal treatment under the law) clause states as follows: "No State shall … deny to any person within its jurisdiction of the equal protection *of the laws*." The key words in this clause are "*of the laws*."

The rights granted by the Fourteenth Amendment are the rights of citizenship, due process and equal treatment *under the law*. But it grants only procedural rights (the ways and means by which the law should be adjudicated or applied) and substantive rights (equal or similar sets of benefits or incentives) under or in lieu of an existing or applicable law. It does not and cannot be used to make law but can only be used to enforce the law after such a law has already been made. It is therefore quite moot on what specific laws it should or should not satisfy. It is not concerned about why a particular law was made; rather its relevance is about how a law has been implemented. A law has to exist before any claim under the equality clause can be granted or legitimized. For instance, in the same way that the equality clause of the Fourteenth Amendment must apply in the case of employment discrimination, there is a law to which it could be referenced: Title V11 of the Civil Rights Act of 1964; it is the same with the Fair Housing Act of 1968. But then to which law does the ruling in *Obergefell v. Hodges* apply, since there is no existing *law* legislated by Congress that would satisfy the remedy being sought? While equal treatment under the law is an acceptable judicial and, one might say, political premise in the United States, it still begs the question: "equal treatment under *which* law?"

It will remain an issue for judicial pundits whether the Fourteenth Amendment by its own text can be arbitrarily used to make law or whether it can grant any specific right other than one tied to an *existing* law. It is for this very reason that Chief Justice Roberts wrote in his dissenting opinion in *Obergefell v. Hodges* same-sex marriage ruling stating, "Do not celebrate the Constitution, it had nothing to do with it," pointing out rather specifically that the remedy sought in this particular case cannot be found or obtained within the *corpus juris* of the Fourteenth Amendment. Justice Scalia joined by Justice Thomas added more scathing remarks to the effect that "the majority had strong-armed its personal values into the Constitution, executing a judicial putsch" (Bravin, 2015, p. A6). Although Justice Kennedy had written for the majority opinion citing constitutional grant of equal dignity, neither the vote nor the opinions expressed have been able to rest due to continuing debate and disagreement on this issue. The "multiplicity of fragmented concepts are used at one and the same time to express rival and incompatible social ideals and policies; they are also used to furnish us with a pluralist political rhetoric whose function is to conceal the depth of our conflicts" (MacIntyre, 1992, p. 62).

In the end, it is equally important to point out that nothing in this argument suggests, let alone implies, any specific inclination for value judgment; what the argument entails is tasking the law and drawing out from it the specificity and meaning of its language. Laws are generally fraught with precedents that oftentimes run contrary to the precise meaning and intent for which they were designed. An example could be the Second Amendment to the US Constitution where an enduring debate persists as to whether it confers individual or collective rights to bear arms—even though the text precisely indicates the right to bear arms in the context of a well-regulated militia. That is why most judicial policy makings rarely escape political judgment; try as hard as we may wish. Because justice as fairness is indivisible and must be seen as an end in itself, it is the principle of unanimity, not majority rule, that can secure justice for all, including the minority. Where this is not tenable, the very idea of using the outcome of a numeric vote to make judicial determination runs afoul of the very intent and essence of justice. Justice itself becomes a victim of political judgment and mathematical reductionism rather than an outcome founded on exhaustive logic and substantive jurisprudence.

Such, therefore, is the case that "where issues of justice are involved, the intensity of desires or the strength of conviction is irrelevant when questions of justice arise" (Rawls, 1971, p. 361); and this particular point applies to majority and minority alike. To the extent that "everything depends on the probable justice of the outcome, the test of constitutional arrangements is always the overall balance of justice" (Rawls, 1971, p. 37). "Democracy and justice are compelling ideas, and many people wish to be associated with those organizations and institutions that provide for democracy and justice. Public institutions and organizations have the highest of purpose—the people's purpose; hence their job is to make the organized achievement of these purposes possible" (Frederickson, 2000, p. 52). Where this balance weighs overwhelmingly in favor of the majority not by the persuasiveness or logic of the argument but simply by virtue of a numeric vote, then justice becomes untenable or is denied.

4 Postmodern Citizenship

Logic and Praxis in State and Identity

The contemporary perception that citizenship may be present in a state without yet being fully developed among its inhabitants is the foundation of the modern sociological theory of citizenship as well as its relationship to public policy. While there have been important structural or systemic limitations on the role of citizens in the governance of contemporary states, social class also serves as a limiting factor that restricts the extent to which one can broadly interpret issues of citizenship, entitlement and obligation. The diversification and individuation of public tastes, lifestyles, cultural history, and ideological differences stand at odds with any assumed political consensus on the status and privileges of citizenship. The combined onslaught of cross-cultural and transnational immigration along with the communicative and integrative role of information technology projects a new portrait of how we will come to experience, in very different ways, the rights and obligations of citizenship both as a collective ideal and as a normative imperative. How we govern as well as relate to each other in our new circumstance will present enormous challenge for governance in the contemporary administrative state.

Epiphenomenalism: Beyond Frameworks and Heuristics

As a means for laying claim to specific kinds of public goods, citizenship can be seen as both a device and an argument. While it can serve as a device for achieving an instrumental as well as a moral end, it can also be used as an argument for justifying several unique sets of entitlements as well as attachment to a particular political community. But then, these do not touch at the core of what the ideal of citizenship should embody. In terms of the relationship between the state and the individual, I see citizenship as having a constitutive quality that results from but at the same time overlaps with the state. In "providing rights, society and the state do not simply give them to citizens gratis; citizens must, on the other hand, subject themselves to the procedures and institutions necessary to ensure that the state can continue to provide rights" (Gorham, 1995, p. 29). Hence, when we say the word 'citizen,' we also imply obligation. To what extent should the state be obligated to its citizens and vice versa?

Because both serve as necessary ingredients for the construction of nationhood, state and citizenship must be seen as mutually reinforcing; the first is concerned with constructing effective institutions and procedures critical for a functional administrative system, while the latter focuses on creating a sense of ownership and commitment anchored on collective interest. "By its actions (rules, regulations, and institutions), the state thus creates awareness within the citizenry of the reciprocal nature of duty, obligation, and responsibility" (Kalu, 2008, p. 13). I argue that what should be more reflective of the ideal of citizenship would depend on the qualities and attitudes that individuals share in common both in their disposition toward the state and in their relationships to one another. These qualities should, in fact, be seen as an integral part of the inchoate political culture. "The citizen has to view himself as playing an active role in determining his society's future, and as taking responsibility for the collective decisions that are made" (Miller, 1992, p. 96).

Hence, what ought to hold the political community together is a kind of consensus on the nature of the collective interest—akin to what Norton Long (1981) refers to as the 'ethical consensus.' It behooves us, therefore, to view citizenship beyond the notion of legal status or entitlement, but also in terms of individual expressions regarding various ethical possibilities and the limitations granted within the state or political community.

The State and the Structure of Identity

From the above analysis, it would be reasonable to make the case that the state provides the structural anchor for the expression of citizenship and in fact forms the value and functional premises upon which it is expressed. To the extent that all aspects of these value premises are universally applicable to other states, does this therefore imply that individuals are citizens only to the extent the state is able to guarantee it? For instance, some states guarantee more freedoms and civil liberties than others: some prefer authoritarian regimes to democratic ones, and others are plainly predatory when it comes to handling matters of state responsibility and citizen interest. On this account alone, states, more or less, offer different guarantees of 'citizenship' to their citizens. By providing a 'shared narrative' of individual experience (Tilly, 1996) which forms 'shared understandings' of a political community (Walzer, 1983), citizenship provides a complex and substantive, though not the only, set of representations of national identity.

As Frederickson (1991, p. 406) points out, "the modern development of citizenship assumes that a vigorous citizenry is compatible with an effective public administration," hence its value rests on enabling those activities that reinforce and at the same time legitimize state authority and action. To the extent that citizenship can be validated in lieu of the state, its identity and characteristics would also depend on the scope of guarantees permissible by the state.

While membership of a state "is an attachment that shapes the very identity that defines us in terms of who we are, it is also a constitutive attachment" (Charney, 2003, pp. 299–300) that for the most part binds each individual to a broader community of citizenship. As a construct, citizenship therefore requires a state to give it character. As a *practice* (engaging in those obligations that validate specific qualities) individuals are in a position to give content and meaning to the broad social and political values attached to citizenship as both status and experience. To this effect, several works on citizenship in political science and sociology seem to demonstrate an acute awareness of the tensions inherent in the interpretations and interdependence of cultural constructions of identity, social relationships, the market and types of political participation (Crouch, Eder and Tambini, 2001; Carens, 2000; Tully, 1995).

Traditionally, the idea of citizenship connotes two main characteristics: legal status (Rubenstein, 2000), and a normative conception of social membership, substantive equality and inclusion (Marshall, 1950; Rubenstein, 2000). Of particular note is the notion that citizenship rights serve to equalize individuals with regard to status, thereby enabling them to participate in the community and to establish a sense of common purpose and loyalty to the community (Marshall, 1965). While the above two conceptions address the legal and normative issues of citizenship that have contributed to the contemporary interpretation and understanding, they still fall short in terms of determining the fundamental principles under which such legal status, individual equality, and community participation transcend identity.

The idea of identity connotes a sense of belongingness or identification with certain values, practices or ideologies. But in its most basic appeal to the state, any construction of identity must reflect the constitutive and communitarian qualities in its understanding, as well as in expression. While civic knowledge of existing norms and values would not be enough, authentication of identity requires that "such knowledge become salient to the individual through the experience of participation in relevant action, through the negotiation of identity with others, and through incorporating narratives about values, selfhood, and national identity into one's self-definition" (Haste, 2004, p. 433).

In the sense that a person's action draws on these values and the underlying guiding principles shared by similarly situated others, and on the recognition that the 'whole is built into the parts and vice versa,' individual expressions of identity require relational reciprocity for their validation. Because individual identity is generally expressed *in lieu* of some other thing else, it represents a microcosm of a much larger construction (collective or group identity), which is necessary for its legitimation at the individual level. One does not identify solely with oneself but only in relation to the others or to something else. Hence, "self and group identity, negotiated through narrative and dialogue as well as through trying to make sense of social structures and representations, are crucial to understanding the construction of the citizen" (Haste, 2004, p. 420). This still leaves us with a peculiar logic that is rarely transcendental.

Critical Social Science and Postmodernity: Competing Narratives

Constructions, assumptions, and argumentation serve important functions in the interpretations necessary for understanding how social and economic roles shape the reality of our human experience in a world of increasing uncertainty and flux. Drawing from an array of theoretical foundations, "critical social theory targets positivism both on the level of everyday life and in social theories that reduce the social world to patterns of cause and effect" (Agger, 1991, p. 109). It aims to go beyond the surface of social life and uncover the assumptions that keep us from a full and true understanding of how the world works and to discover ways to change or redirect it toward its ontological nature. "Its proponents seek to reveal society for what it is, to unmask its essence and mode of operation, and to lay the foundations for emancipation through deep-seated social change" (Tosi, 2009, p. 233). In this regard, "a good deal of social science logic has been challenged for lacking the sort of dialectical imagination that enables social scientists to look beyond the appearance of given social facts toward new social facts" (Agger, 1991, p. 109).

As critical theorists (Adorno, 1984; Horkheimer, 1972; Marcuse, 1978; Habermas, 1979) sought a reconstruction of the logic and method of orthodox Marxism to fit it more properly to emerging social facts of contemporary society, they also reinforced a level of skepticism that questioned the relevance of citizenship as a social status. While Marx held the view that what really matters to people is the world of work and immediate personal relationships as opposed to social status, critical theorists maintain that the truth of the human condition lies in the act of relative discovery—each man for himself in his own world of experience. Drawn from this premise, postmodernism has been "marked by the renunciation of foundational thought, of rules governing art, and of the ideological discourses relative to liberalism and Marxism" (Aronowitz, 1989, p. 46). Although liberalism and Marxism emphasize the structural role of social class and the mechanisms of production as foundational elements in state formation and social organization, postmodernists argue that "what has so far been taken as privileged discourse is merely a construction that conceals power and self-interest" (Aronowitz, 1989, pp. 55–56). As "disparate elements of contemporary social change give way to a range of labels, including postindustrialism, postmaterialism, post-Fordism, disorganized capitalism, and information society" (Gilbert, 1992, p. 52), postmodernism has become the collective identification that captures the essence of these new developments.

Hence, rather than searching for laws that guide action, "the postmodern theorist is committed to framing propositions that together constitute a working model tailored to an empirically verifiable situation" (Aronowitz, 1989, p. 56)—that is tied to the reality of individual experience, sense-making and interpretation. To the extent that life in the West is increasingly characterized by "a pervasive informationalism, fragmented organizational forms, and by views of knowledge which dissolve history's grand narratives; the importance of postmodernism in the construction of citizenship lies not in the objective forms of media, technology, or information, but in how they are appropriated into new modes of experience and expression—how they shape identity" (Gilbert, 1992, p. 54; Lyotard, 1984).

Citizenship is one among many identities an individual will feel. While it is distinguished by being necessary for moral maturity, and by its potential to moderate the divisiveness of other identity feelings—gender, religion, race, class and nation—it helps to reinforce specific attitudes and behaviors expected of citizens (Gilbert, 1992, p. 52). However, whatever universality or commonness the concept may have is being rapidly weakened by a series of tensions—"incompatible pairs of definitions, individual freedom versus social duties and obligations, the conflict between the private and the public citizen, the difficulties of incorporating a complex society into a coherent relationship with a unitary polity, and the conflicting demand of state and world citizenship" (Heater, 1990, p. 284). Nonetheless, the postmodern experience constitutes a diversification of social worlds each with its own codes of behavior, its scenes, economies and pleasures; for those who have access to them they do provide space in which to assert some choice and control over everyday life (Gilbert, 1992, p. 55).

Critical reflection is not an absolute origin but is dependent on something prior, which it takes as its object while simultaneously originating from it (McCarthy, 1996, p. 79). However, the logic of citizenship is drawn on the premise that, while the natural consciousness of the everyday life world in which we find ourselves is already a given, phenomenological reflection traces its own origins through the successive stages of the manifestation of consciousness (McCarthy, 1996, p. 79). For instance, *Phenomenology Online* (2015) explains that there is a difference between our pre-reflective lived understanding of the *meaning* of time and a self-reflective grasp of the phenomenological structure of the *lived meaning* of time. To get at the latter is a difficult and often laborious task, involving a process of reflectively appropriating, clarifying and making explicit the aspects of the meaning of the lived experience. That is, we discover the ideal of citizenship through its own lived experience.

While most explorations of citizenship in the contemporary era are less optimistic in the face of the difficulties of reversing the fragmenting and nihilistic tendencies of postmodern society (Gilbert, 1992), the more enduring threat to citizenship lies in the dominance of an intrusive kind of consumerist market liberalism and in the loss of individual moral authority in the face of the media's ever-changing (and illusory) rendition of the world (Wexler, 1990). Critical theorists will accept a notion of citizenship that leads to more freedom (is emancipatory) as opposed to one that is restrictive and dominated by the legal and institutional structures of the state. But then, they see it not as an absolute or an embodiment of the truth that it pretends to be, but as something that requires continuous investigation and discovery. They worry about the implied inequalities inherent in deliberative democracies and how these are manifested in the class-based social systems of political and economic relationships.

As we continue to redefine the world around us, we also (perhaps unknowingly) construct abstract little spaces of 'imaginary publics' barely large enough to accommodate the kind of democratic discourse necessary to facilitate participatory citizenship in the Aristotelian tradition. We end up creating what Wexler (1990) refers to as the 'semiotic society,' or what Sementelli (2009) calls the 'phantom public'—in which "the very idea of citizenship is easily co-opted into the superficial and diffused network of relations of contact, rather than the identity that might result from the solidarity of contract" (Wexler, 1990; Gilbert,

1992, p. 60). While this is not the kind of civic society that is amenable to postmodernist thinking in the conventional sense of the term, ironically, its emphasis on seeking different and alternate paths to self-expression seem to magnify the thing it wishes to avoid. In Foucauldian terms, it helps to reinforce "identities and differences—elements of the self that constitute the civilization to which it is subject" (Gorham, 1995, p. 45).

Postmodern Intentionality: Emancipatory Discourse as Meaning

Postmodernism is a reactionary movement to the validity or 'truthfulness' of the existence of universal principles. While it maintains an antifoundational sentiment, it at the same time seeks a repudiation "of 'certainties' or universalizations in science, philosophy, religion, opinion, the arts, and morality" (Carlton, 2006, p. 188). By rejecting the "kinds of 'totalizing narratives' that claims to govern complex fields of social activity and social representation, the postmodernist rejects the possibility of knowing the past, because history is fragmented and relative" (Carlton, 2006, pp. 188–189). It holds that because there are "no set of ultimate standards, hence all 'grand narratives' are suspect; and all traditions have to be seriously questioned and perhaps abandoned altogether" (Carlton, 2006, p. 186). Rather, social life operates on the logic of discontinuities, paradoxes, ironies and differences. These, therefore, must be appreciated, even celebrated if we are to be able to capture real truth in both form and content. Reason is one *form* of a larger grand narrative that can be broken into various parts, because there are different currents or paths for developing the *will* to knowledge. Reason, therefore, is constitutive because it derives *from itself* that which we can recognize only after it has escaped from *itself*. Considered as a process, values harbor an element of indeterminacy and non-permanency; but it depends on "how they are used, invoked, negotiated, and managed in dialogue between persons and in the individual's interaction with a situation" (Haste, 2004, p. 422).

The postmodern culture of 'anything goes,' and the inclination to seek the truth by negating the very historical foundation upon which we form our own abstract notion of what the truth may be, reflects a quest for knowledge that is nether technical nor pragmatic but emancipatory. They seek continual novelty on the excuse that since "we are already caught within the infinite displacement of images we should swim buoyantly in that flow rather than seeking firm ground" (Kolb, 1990, p. 100). Postmodernists deny the existence of a shared objective reality. They claim that different cultural groups live in different realities, hence a people's reality is only its *perception* or *interpretation* of the external world and is not the world itself. Therefore, we are really creating truth as we interpret, but certainly not discovering it (Rorty, 1989). They also contend that a thing is true because I *believe it*; but I *do not believe it* because it is true, since neither possibility can be apriorily known to be certain.

One can therefore draw on the analogy of the stage in Jacques Derrida's *The Theater of Cruelty*. For Derrida, "the stage is theological for as long as it is dominated by speech, by a will to speech, by the layout of a primary logos which does not belong to the theatrical site but governs it from a distance" (Derrida, 1978, p. 235). We therefore end up constructing a mute stage, despite the presence of actors and performers, but yet, one whose clamor for recognition has not yet been pacified into words. The public sphere is a mute stage with citizens represented as actors, and the state, though not physically present, can make its will felt through the unspoken words of the law. In this encounter and although the state sets "the general structure in which each agency (citizen) is linked to all the others by representation, the irrepresentability of the individual present is thus dissimulated, suppressed or dissolved within the infinite chain or representations" (Derrida, 1978, p. 253). In this regard, citizenship limits individual expression and autonomy by absorbing both the public and private spheres into a realm controlled from without.

But to envisage the ideal of citizenship in the lonely isolation of individual thought and rationality broadly construed is to misunderstand its practical and reciprocal qualities. It is the equivalence of holding out the promise that "cultural movements originate in the free will of subjects who act as independent historical and moral agents" (Schulte-Sasse, 1986, p. 7). By constructing words, symbols and signs phrased in semantic esotericisms, rational will formation becomes increasingly difficult when language loses its ability to communicate discrete real-world experiences (Fox, 1996). "Worse, symbols interacting in hyperspace without benefit of mooring in work-a-day reality can only come back around to distort any reform of that reality" (Fox, 1996, p. 257).

The postmodern narrative is bereft of context and body, in the sense that what we have is a situation where citizenship is constructed in the abstract as a form of consciousness. Citizenship is seen as a mindset that when collectively expressed transcends a consciousness that sets in motion the very social processes (protests, movements, public opinion and people willingly paying their taxes) that drives collective action. It is a self-referential power that operates on a logic that exists outside of the very source from which it emanates. In this regard, citizenship can be expressed anywhere, any time and under uniquely different situations, and therein lies the problem of postmodern deconstructivism. By delinking citizenship from the state and transforming it into a state of mind, it loses body and context. As René Descartes would argue, it is difficult for the soul to move itself except in its association with the body, and our knowledge of the soul does not exist, in and of itself; it lacks corporeality but is expressed only in the way it directs the actions of the body.

As a social phenomenon, citizenship represents a framework around which specific political and social relations are organized—but in such a way that, on the one hand, it is validated as a collective norm and on the other, as a legitimating activity. But when exposed to different interpretations, worldviews or sense making as in the postmodernist context, it loses its essential quality as a binding force that undergirds evolving reciprocal relationships between state and citizen. Henri Foucault's conceptualization of power can serve as a fitting analogy to the postmodern conceptualization of citizenship. For Foucault (Rabinow, 1991), power is an everyday socialized and embodied phenomenon that transcends politics. It is a major source of social discipline and conformity, diffused and embodied in discourse, knowledge, and 'regimes of truth,' hence what makes us who we are. Power is constituted through accepted forms of knowledge, scientific understanding and truth. Conceived in the Foucauldian discourse on power relationships in society as expressed through language and practices, and just like power, citizenship is a "form of rationality which can rule and regulate, dominating and imposing its rationality upon the totality of the social body" (Foucault, 1988, p. 38).

As a phenomenon, Foucault's 'power' pervades society and is constantly being renegotiated and changed. In the same way, citizenship as a cognitive construct is also constantly being redefined and renegotiated according to the existing 'regimes of truth.' Power and citizenship are functional in the sense that both can set in motion various social and political processes that can change the nature and structure of social relations in unexpected ways. Equally, citizenship is viewed as an interpretive journey in which individuals interpret the past, recognize the universal linguistic character of their relationship to the world, re-examine their traditions, accept or reject social practices and recognize the importance of memories in their interpretation and assessment of the present (Alejandro, 1993, p. 36). In this context, citizenship thus offers a collective space and understanding where individuals are able to share the experience "not as a juridical category or a collection of civic attitudes, but as a *hermeneutic horizon*, a practice, or even textual reality" (Alejandro 1993, 37). What is meant by *hermeneutic horizon* is "a world nurtured by traditions, institutions and practices with open boundaries for reflection" (Alejandro, 1993, p. 37). While a hermeneutic perspective conceives of the public sphere as a space of fluidity, contingency and equality, it is also a space for different voices, languages and silences (Alejandro, 1993, p. 223). It is a space for airing problems and resolving conflicts in the mutual aspiration for the common good.

Norm-Building, Frame-Bending: The Ethos of Deconstructionism

The paradoxical nature of citizenship lies in the fact that it has been a key nexus for creating both equality (in terms of rights) and inequality (in terms of differences in socioeconomic status). As we analyze the various conceptions of citizenship in light of historical continuities and change in the postmodern environment, we should also recognize how these manifest themselves in new forms of identity and social organization. As the conceptualization of citizenship becomes diffused, as demographic and cultural realignments change the face of major communities and urban centers and as our responsibilities and unity of purpose change and grow over time, "this very increase brings with it a danger that our personal sense of duty and obligation may also diminish" (Matheson, 1897, p. 32).

Postmodern thinking has opened up a Pandora's Box of skepticism and rejectionism with an end that is oftentimes illusory and indeterminate. To seek the deconstruction of traditional institutions and structures that have withstood the test of time, simply for the thrill of a possible end that is neither here nor there, would seem to undermine the whole essence of objective rationality. Like ideology, the postmodern argument claims, ironically, "to unify and render manageable a social universe which because of the evident loss of worldliness has become increasingly chaotic and incomprehensible to its inhabitants" (Hansen, 1993, pp. 116–117). To the extent that it reflects the cognitive aspect of genuine worldliness, it offers a way for humans in their own respective selves to transform the chaotic and accidental into the patterned and explicable (Hansen, 1993, p. 117).

Inspired, on the one hand, by the increasing level of globalization and, on the other, by transnational immigration and a world without borders, many scholars have started to mute the idea of global citizenship. This explanation comes in many coinages such as post-sovereign citizenship, post-nationalism and cultural citizenship (Stevenson, 1997; Halliday, 2000; Schneider, 2000; Murphy and Harty, 2003; Gifford, 2004)—all of which further "complicate the notion of citizenship as membership in the community in which one is born or lives" (Glenn, 2000, p. 10). "As the world grows more interconnected in a huge number of ways, as political jurisdictions become more encompassing and political institutions more vertically structured (i.e., European Union, World Trade Organization, etc.), and as many types of economic inequality mount, democratic citizenship increasingly becomes far more a legitimating slogan than a lived reality for most citizens" (Smith, 2005, p. 681). To the extent that citizenship provides a forum where people transcend their differences and think about the common good of all citizens (Cairns, 1993; Kymlicka, 1995, p. 175), it cannot perform its vital integrative function if it is group-differentiated. It ceases to be a device to cultivate a sense of community and a common sense of purpose (Heater, 1990, p. 295).

Another issue about globalization is whether the 'nation-state' is still the relevant entity for grounding rights and responsibilities and whether such a development would represent a shift from a nation-based (citizen-based) notion of rights to a more individual-based notion of universal rights (Glenn, 2000, pp. 13–14). While the idea of universal rights and a repudiation of the state seem to have opened a loophole that fired much of the value deconstructionism engaged by postmodernists, predictions surrounding the demise of the state abound. For the moment, "the 'nation-state' remains the primary vehicle in the enforcement of any universally defined rights, even in matters dealing with international conventions" (Glenn, 2000, p. 14). Even if the postmodern deontological argument sounds plausible, its latent attempt to challenge the sovereign and regulatory authority of the state also implies a repudiation (or rather deconstruction) of the structural and normative basis of citizenship without offering a more *functional* or replacement alternative.

As the rise of group-based claims further erode the sense of shared civic purpose and solidarity within liberal democracies (Kymlicka, 1995), the prospects of recovering traditional forms of identity and virtuous citizenship in our postmodern condition could become more elusive. What accounts for the seeming contestability of citizenship is not a lack of awareness or experience of it at the individual or community level but rather the epistemological deconstructions and reconstructions surrounding the term. These accounts and others have shaped the tension underpinning the contemporary crisis in culture between seemingly extant traditionalism and an unsettled postmodern dogmatism, in the ideological "quest for total control, or rationalization of social and political life—and of history itself" (Hansen, 1993, p. 118).

Fox and Miller (1995, p. 45) put it more succinctly to the effect that "postmodernism has come to represent the return and revenge of the different, the assertion of the random nonpattern and the unassimilable anomaly." In the continuing effort to "splice and tape cultural identities so that any reassuring sense of fixity or essence is subverted" (Beiner, 2003, p. 27), the apparent postmodern skepticism regarding all forms of rationality brings us no comfort or closure in the sense that its own view (if any) about where the ultimate truth may lie is also in doubt. The result has been the rise of alternative cultures, romanticization of language, interpretive relativism as a new moral fabric, the rationalization of the profane, the celebration of vice, and the endless rupture of tradition to which the contemporary world is now exposed—most of which have little or no phenomenological grounding in history and in existing social practices.

5 Stateness, Identity and Leadership

A Discourse

A central problem in citizenship theory is the tendency to generate parallel interpretations that are mutually self-reinforcing. Because citizenship transcends both the universality of rights and the pragmatism of individual obligation, it implies on the one hand the recognition of a universal principle and on the other a form of social contract between the state and the individual. The true meaning of citizenship falls apart when one or both of these requirements are not fulfilled. Furthermore, conceiving of citizenship within the limits of a state's political framework that could also make the exercise of rights and obligations structurally difficult would seem to undermine the liberal-pluralist view of citizenship common among democratic *polities*.

There are two main reasons for this. Most contemporary analyses of what the construct means have over the years become increasingly reductionist by focusing more and more on personal experiences and the limits of public authority. Furthermore, a blurring of the line regarding the mutual obligation between the state and citizen has evolved—in terms of the state's ensuring access to public goods and opportunity for all, and citizens' fulfilling those obligations that grant legitimacy to the institutional role and authority of the state, such as paying taxes, voting in elections and serving on the jury when called upon to do so. Much of this is equally due to the functional ambiguities that some have associated to the emergence of the *hollow state* (Milward, Provan and Else, 1993; Milward and Provan, 2000; Klijn, 2002; Terry, 2005; Frederickson and Frederickson, 2007).

The Nation and State: Extending the Narrative

It is by design that I did not use the commonly referenced twin denotation of "nation-state." I prefer to separate the two terms as a way of reinforcing the point that they are essentially different, although the two may occupy the same geopolitical space. Unlike the state, which is anchored on a territorial and geopolitical foundation, a nation is a cultural embodiment that transcends "not merely an extended web of relationships between those who share a certain identity; it also involves a conception of the community to which the members of the nation belong" (Poole, 1999, p. 69). Culturally, various states are *multinational* or multicultural (like the United States) while others are *mononational* or *monocultural* (like Japan). "For much of the modern world, the nation has appropriated to itself the linguistic and cultural means necessary for the articulation of the sense of self of its members" (Poole, 1999, p. 69), thus oftentimes conflating "national identity" as synonymous with identification to state and country. This confusion is quite evident in the body politic, when pursuit of the political interest of group identity trumps the political interest of common citizenship and statehood, sometimes with disastrous consequences.

Alternatively, the state is an ideal form of society; integrated by possessing a coercive authority legally supreme over any individual or group that is part of the society (Laski, 1935, p. 8). "It has acquired the license of sovereignty over a territory as well as supremacy over all other forms of association because it is formally competent to bind them to obedience without itself being bound" (Laski, 1935, p. 10). The irony of the modern state is that "while it may, in fact, be unwise or unjust in what it commands; neither unwisdom nor injustice makes any difference to the formal legal right of the state to exact and enforce obedience to its orders" (Laski, 1935, p. 10). In whatever way it may appeal to us, the state and citizens are mutually reinforcing, if for no other reason than that citizenship, while it involves a kind of sustained relationship with the *others,* requires a foundational framework upon which such relationship could be, more or less, freely expressed.

Equally important is that in almost every modern state, especially in plural political systems, the structure of identity comes in multiple dimensions, such as national, group, associational, ethnic, gender, sexual, religious, professional, socioeconomic identities, *ad infinitum*. In the ensuing plethora of identities, we end up losing or, at best, introducing a series of conceptual ambiguities in the way we conceive of the purpose and practice of citizenship. The scope of loyalty necessary to maintain a common ethos of nationhood and community within the citizenry is also undermined. Although identity formation is a process that, more often than not, begins outside the perspective of legal rules and regulations, it is often drawn into the legal and political fields (Isin and Wood, 1999, p. 19). Hence, "although political leaders may suggest that the state is the only legitimate source of authority to establish rules for social behavior, in fact other organizations may set the effective rules of the game in opposition to those put forth by the state" (Migdal 2001, p. 190). Potentially, the public space becomes an arena of competing sets of principles and values that, in some ways, may create perpetual conflict and acrimony to the detriment of the unifying virtues we mostly associate with the ideal of common citizenship.

The emphasis on identity is a recognition of the similarities and distinctiveness in the common properties or interests that may exist between individuals. But when such identifications become deindividualized and morphed into a group form, they turn into a forum for making specific group claims and rights that may be inimical to the type of collective human flourishing critical for attaining the good life for all. While this point could equally be argued the other way round, the ensuing "tension between the universal aspirations of citizenship and the particularistic claims of identity" (Isin and Wood, 1999, p. 20) makes it more difficult to know whether specific claims for recognition and rights are based on the status and rights claims of universal citizenship or on specific group identities independent of existing citizenship rights. In this context, citizenship must of necessity harbor two competing properties: inclusion and exclusion, both equally tolerated as expressions of rights and freedoms no matter how contradictory.

Citizenship, Market Economy and Welfare State

The capacity of the modern state to handle all of its citizens' problems may have reached its boiling point and this in light of an increasing "awareness of a series of new and formidable challenges the scope of which plainly extends far beyond national boundaries and effectively ensures that they cannot be successfully met within such boundaries" (Dunn, 1995, pp. 4–5). As we expect the state to solve all of mankind's problems—political, economic, environmental, demographic, epidemiological, refugee and transborder immigration—it has become obvious that the free-market system, left alone, is incapable of addressing these and may have, in fundamental ways, made them worse. While the competitive spirit of the market economy oftentimes creates winners and losers, the ensuing socioeconomic classification and burden-shifting as a result of market failures becomes the responsibility of the state and through it of the taxpayers. The welfare state therefore has become an adjustment mechanism to address the failure of the market to ensure an equitable, or rather fair, distribution of goods and services as well as economic opportunities for all citizens. But at what cost?

By mediating the nature of the relationship between the state and citizen, the welfare state redefines the scope and parameters of the expression of individual autonomy. The restrictive and rule-bound character of state paternalism defeats the central purpose of individual freedom and choice. Because of the "tendency to individualize social problems and their treatment, current displacements in social policies and services risk undermining their crucial links to citizenship" (Procacci, 2001, p. 49). Because much of these displacements are shaped by economic considerations and perennial fiscal crisis within liberal economies, "the task therefore remains one of finding a way for addressing problems of inequality in a society of equals" (Procacci, 2001, p. 52). State economic or redistributive policies should thus be guided first by an understanding as to whether the market economy is conditioned upon the welfare state or whether the welfare state is a consequence of the market system. While the policy tools may be different under each of the above scenarios, they provide a basis for elevating the welfare state to the status of a right of citizenship.

Alternatively and in many developed countries, the welfare system did not arise out of any universal principles of right; it is a state response to social problems and a way of extending public goods and opportunity to those who may not have it at one point in time or another. Considered in light of the free-market regime, the welfare system has become one of a few other channels through which industrialized states redress fundamental redistributive issues of domestic policy and inequality. While it may suggest a sense of entitlement on the part of potential beneficiaries, the welfare system recreates our notion of citizenship. However, "despite all its efforts to bring about a greater measure of individual social security, the welfare state has not helped to create a strong, self-confident sense of identity among its individual citizens" (Kroes, 2000, p. 109). Although it may serve the purpose of social citizenship, it does not *ipso facto* imply or guarantee political citizenship.

Nonetheless, the idea of social citizenship "implies that if governments try to cut the welfare state, they will confront resistance based upon a belief that people have rights embedded in welfare services which no one ought to tamper with" (King and Waldron, 1988, p. 417). When viewed in this light, the welfare system becomes an instrument through which specific social rights of citizenship can be secured, but the problem of the welfare state is that it does not address the kind of rough equality in terms of political rights desired among citizens of the state. It seeks, instead, to reshape our understanding of citizenship as a reciprocal activity between the state and the individual—a kind of new paternalism anchored on what is generally understood as welfare contractualism. However, welfare contractualism and the notion of social citizenship are different. While "welfare contractualism makes the payment of a publicly-financed minimum income (welfare) to the individual conditional on his or her satisfying specific behavioral requirements—such as active job search, retraining or work itself—social citizenship as manifested in a range of social rights has a quality of unconditionality to it" that ought to be protected (White, 2000, p. 509). It is only when social citizenship is reinforced by political citizenship that individuals are in a better position "to challenge or defend the existing distribution of property and interest and to bring their own judgments on public issues" (King and Waldron, 1988, pp. 426–427).

In classic Aristotelian logic, the emphasis on participatory citizenship was a way of establishing the primacy of politics in civic life and a type of social organization that would contribute to the good life and entitlement within the *polis*. While most liberal democratic states are able to accord their citizens the freedom to participate (or not to participate), ironically, we find that "democratic citizenship in its contemporary form does not seem to encourage [a] high level of involvement or devotion" (Walzer, 1989, p. 219) in political or civic affairs. Amid a series of other commitments and demands of modern society, individuals have come to develop conflicting obligations as well as competing priorities. Besides the evident low voter turnout in many modern societies, there is a growing detachment from the type of virtue citizenship that Aristotle demanded.

In our contemporary experience, "citizenship is unlikely to be the primary identity or the consuming passion of men and women living in complex and highly differentiated societies—where politics competes for time and attention with class, ethnicity, religion and family—and where these latter four do not draw people together but rather separate and divide them" (Walzer, 1989, p. 218). As globalization continues to generate radical transformations in the welfare state, individuals have "attempted to construct meanings of citizenship beyond the national sphere in the face of multi-and-interculturalism and cross-cutting legal dimensions" (Eley and Palmowski, 2004). This raises a crucial question: Can postmodern thinking reconcile "the tensions inherent in the interdependence of cultural constructions of identity, social relationships, and the market" (Eley and Palmowski, 2004)? How would it transcend the classical and contemporary views of citizenship and political participation?

Gandhi: Leadership as Citizenship-in-Action

This discussion views citizenship as both an expression and a form of engagement, as a means to an end but not necessarily as an end in itself. Although we have construed citizenship as having an active dimension (when people pay their taxes, vote in elections, and engage in public service or philanthropy) and a passive dimension (when people decide not to actively participate in public deliberations, refuse to vote, are disenchanted with conventional political processes, free ride on the efforts of others, and demonstrate resigned indignation to issues of state and political governance), there are other expressions of citizenship that do not fit so nicely into the above two categories. I regard this third element as the *contingent* dimension—that is an aspect of citizenship and rights that, although not yet tied to a state, has acquired the moral legitimacy that warrants its universal recognition. "It demonstrates how a symbol (citizenship), in a rather slow but gradual process, is translated into political action, and finally into the law of the land and eventually into an important instrument of political change—into a legal and political reality" (Gross, 1999, p. 79). "If citizenship involves the struggle for membership and participation in the community, then its analysis should necessitate examining the way in which different groups, classes, and movements struggle to gain degrees of autonomy and control over their lives in the face of various forms of stratification and political oppression" (Held, 1989, p. 199).

On the premise that "the ability of individuals or groups to express their opposition to the policies pursued by governments and organizations in the public or private sectors is an important aspect of liberal democratic states" (Joyce, 2002, p. 15), it is equally the case that "the rights of peaceful protest and assembly are among the fundamental freedoms that distinguish a free society from a totalitarian one" (Home Office, 1985, p. 2; Joyce, 2002, p. 15). As a way of further illuminating the practicality of this narrative, I will digress a bit with an illustration of leadership as *citizenship-in-action* and as a movement. I discuss the political struggles of Gandhi as an expression of *contingent citizenship* (before India became independent) and *active citizenship* (after India became independent). The beginning of Gandhi's political activism epitomized a citizen without a state, in the sense that he had an idea of a prospective association with a state, and it was that expectation that drove his brand of leadership and nonviolent movement. His was a movement to validate the essence of Indian statehood and its sovereign and mutual obligation to all of its citizens. How did he do it, and what type of leadership and citizenship-in-action made this possible? Like many before him, Gandhi was the consummate citizen.

Mohandas Karamchand Gandhi was born on October 2, 1869, in Porbandar, India. Gandhi led the effort to free India from British rule through nonviolent resistance and is generally seen as the father of the post-independent Indian nation. He left the shores of India on September 4, 1887, to study law in London. Although he returned to India in 1891 to practice, he was to take a one-year contract to do legal work in South Africa, which was then also controlled by the British. When he attempted to claim his rights as a British subject he was abused and soon saw that all Indians suffered similar treatment. Although he stayed in

South Africa for 21 years working to secure rights for Indian people, he developed a method of action based upon the principles of courage, nonviolence and truth called *Satyagraha*.[1]

On May 22, 1894, Gandhi established the Natal Indian Congress and worked diligently to expand its membership to all classes and castes. While he became well known for his activism, he had also in a few short years become a leader of the Indian community in South Africa. In 1896, when he traveled to India to raise support for the Natal Indian Congress, he pointed out that:

> *Our method in South Africa is to conquer hatred by love; we do not attempt to have individuals punished but as a rule, patiently suffer wrongs at their hands. Generally, our prayers are not to demand compensation for past injuries, but to render a repetition of those injuries impossible and to remove the causes.*
>
> Tidrick, 2006, p. 56

For Gandhi, *Satyagraha* promoted nonviolence and civil disobedience as the most appropriate methods for achieving political and social goals. While "the aim of civil disobedience is to draw public attention to the objectives of the group or to clarify the nature of the conflict" (Carter, 1983, p. 15), it may also "further serve to establish a sense of solidarity among the members of the movement" (Joyce, 2002, p. 59), especially when it is motivated by moral, religious or political impulses (Walzer, 1970, p. 4).

In 1915, he returned to India and within 15 years became the leader of the Indian nationalist movement. On arrival back to India, Gandhi was not impressed by the degree of suffering among the farmers and the Indian peasantry as a whole. He led a series of campaigns in support of strike action by Indian workers and freed political prisoners held by the colonial authority. Using the principles of nonviolent disobedience, Gandhi led the campaign for Indian Independence from Britain. Although he was arrested many times by the British authorities for his activities in South Africa and India, he sincerely believed that it was honorable to go to jail for a just cause. He would later spend seven years in prison for his political activities.[2] As a strategy he used fasting and self-denial as symbolic ways to impress upon others the need to be nonviolent. As the human symbol of the struggle for Indian independence, he exuded virtue, and his simplistic lifestyle and minimal dress code endeared him to the people. Dressing in all-local attire, which also signaled a profound change of thought and action, symbolized a one-man 'protest' movement.

For a professional lawyer who had been exposed to British education and civilization in the formative years of his adulthood, he knew that he could reach the 'souls' of the masses and the poor by looking and living just like them. The art of "going native," thus became a virtue as well as a moral calling—a genuine reawakening of the "Indian" in him, as opposed to the enlightened British 'subject.' As a mobilizer and as one who inspired others into action, Gandhi wanted two kinds of followers (see Tidrick, 2006, p. 126): a relatively small group of helpers (whom he referred to as 'co-workers') who like himself were committed to getting people on the road to true self-rule and a necessarily larger group that was capable of the moral awakening he and his co-workers were trying to bring about. They would offer themselves up for sacrifice, not in obedience to a mere human leader, but to the inner moral promptings that the leader had inspired. They would act, that is to say, in response to God's command. In 1947, India was granted Independence and was partitioned into two countries: India and Pakistan. Fatefully, Gandhi was assassinated in 1948 by a Hindu fanatic.

From the outset, Gandhi's leadership development as a child of circumstance was evident, as a result of early exposure to British education and culture, his activities in South Africa and his pioneering role as activist in the struggle to initiate a process that would eventually bring an end to the British Colonial Empire beyond the borders of his native India. The impact of his leadership, therefore, was as local as it was global. Three theoretical models are relevant in any analysis of Gandhi's leadership: charismatic, situational and transformational. To the extent that he embraced all three models, it is also necessary to evaluate his leadership qualities on the basis of the following criteria: personality, context and process (Figure 5.1). On the general premise that a strategic leader is one who has acquired experience through practice in planning, directing, supporting, motivating and mentoring subordinates toward the accomplishment of stated objectives, these activities were very much attributable to Gandhi. To the extent that he saw leadership as a shared responsibility between himself and his subordinates, he was equally a strategic leader.

Judged on the basis of the characteristics delineated in Figure 5.1, Gandhi had a charismatic personality. Charisma is a Greek word that stands for 'divinely inspired gift.' "It is a term used to describe a form of influence based not on traditional authority but rather on follower perceptions that the leader is endowed with exceptional qualities" (Yukl, 2010, p. 261). According to Max Weber (1947), charisma occurs during social crisis, when a leader emerges with a radical vision that offers a solution to the crisis and attracts followers who believe in the vision. As the followers experience some successes that make the vision appear attainable, they come to perceive the leader as extraordinary. As a trait, charisma, therefore, can be a result of natural attributes or personality.

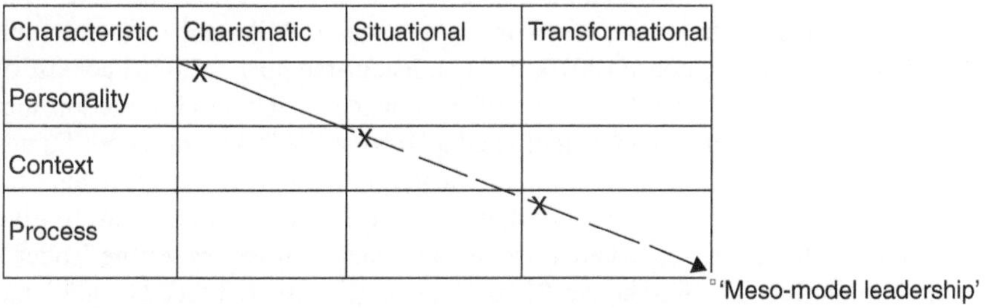

Figure 5.1 Building Blocks of Gandhi's Citizen Leadership: A Multidimensional Approach.

Although a man of diminutive frame, Gandhi's charisma was more about his style than any other physical quality. He was very spiritual, humble and ascetic and lived a very simple life quite different from his earlier experience in British social circles. He exuded awe through self-denial (part of his philosophy of renunciation), which, invariably, made him be revered by his fellow Indians and the international community. He was successful in selling an ideal (suffering and nonviolence) in which his own image and symbolisms (local dress, barefoot, vegetarian, being seen with the poor and underprivileged) became the selling point and, in fact, justification for Indian Independence as an issue of universal rights and justice. Therefore 'suffering for a cause' in the name of *justice* transformed Gandhi as the *cause celebre* of Indian nationalism.

It is also possible to point out that to the extent that he was revered by his subordinates and countrymen, Gandhi had referrent power. The concept of power is related to leadership because it is part of the influence process—the ability to influence others' beliefs, attitudes and courses of action (Northouse, 2010, p. 7). Because referent power is based on an individual's personality, it is possible that it played a greater role in Gandhi's leadership effectiveness (more than charisma) in mobilizing his nation toward a common cause. Gandhi built enduring greatness through a blend of personal humility and spiritual will. The imagery of a British-trained lawyer forsaking (and purposefully denying himself) all the 'good' things in life for the sake of his nation's liberation seemed all-too-consuming for the average Indian (and, in fact, the world) to behold.

It is equally safe to say that there probably would not have been a 'Gandhi' had India achieved its Independence much earlier before he arrived in South Africa. If Gandhi had not been in South Africa in 1894, he would not have been in a position to form the Natal Indian Congress—which, invariably, set the stage for his eventual political activism and organizational ability. The situation that Gandhi met was one of discrimination and mistreatment of Indians in South Africa. His repudiation and resentment of this development created in him a sense of urgency to the effect that the whole Indian nation (still under British colonial rule) was in a similar situation of bondage, exploitation and mistreatment by the British colonial regime. It was therefore the situation/context (the quest for India's Independence) that *created* Gandhi, and he dutifully rose to the occasion to lead a movement to its resolution. India became independent in 1947.

There were two sets of contingency or situational/contextual variables that worked in Gandhi's favor: leader-member relations (LMR) and task structure. As pointed out by Northouse (2010, p. 112), leader-member relations consist of the group atmosphere and the degree of confidence, loyalty and attraction that followers have for their leader. Gandhi had a positive LMR with his subordinates or followers. While "task structure is the degree to which the requirements of a task are clear and spelled out; tasks that are completely structured tend to give more control to the leader, whereas vague and unclear tasks lessen the leader's control and influence" (Northouse, 2010, p. 112). The task that faced Gandhi and his subordinates (the quest for India's Independence) was well-structured and clear. It was a task in which all the participants had a mutually driven cultural and ideological interest.

Transformational leadership is a "process whereby a person engages with others and creates a connection that raises the level of motivation and morality in both the leader and the follower" (Northouse, 2010, p. 172). Transformational leaders go beyond basic emotions such as fear, jealousy, or greed to appeal to such ideals and moral values as justice and liberty (Hunt, 1996, p. 187); this makes them effective at motivating followers to act in ways that support the greater good rather than their own self-interests (Kuhnert, 1994). "Such aligning of individual self-interests and collective interests is a key task of transformational leadership" (Pawar and Eastman, 1997, p. 95). While Gandhi exhibited various aspects of transformational leadership, the issue of Indian Independence was framed as a matter of justice and rights, freedom, poverty and human suffering. By localizing the struggle, Gandhi made sure that every Indian became a stakeholder in the objective (quest for India's Independence) and the process used in its advocacy (nonviolent disobedience). Through spiritual education and teachings, Gandhi personified an embodiment of virtue. His ascetic and simple lifestyle and ready willingness to be jailed for the cause demonstrated a level of fearlessness, unselfishness and self-sacrifice that was unique.

For Gandhi, leadership is about managing the task (objective), the people (participants) and the situation (context). His was an act of leading-by-doing that can also be explained by way of meso-leadership. A meso-leadership paradigm seeks to illustrate the importance of integrating micro-level and macro-level attributes. It seeks to explore the unique cross-level, interactive and reciprocal effects of environmental, organizational, network, group, dyadic and individual-level variables with leadership processes (Gardner and Cogliser, 2009, p. 497). A central assertion, therefore, is that the organizational context impacts leader and member behaviors and vice versa—such that macro phenomena surface from the interaction of micro-level behaviors (Gardner and Cogliser, 2009, p. 497). Gandhi's leadership attributes cannot be fully explained under one model of leadership (charismatic, situational or transformational), but at the more embracing meso level.

Gandhi's political journey offers a crucial lesson in political citizenship. It also reminds us that the "moral legitimacy of any political society depends entirely on consent to the social contract and the obligations that citizens voluntarily assume when they agree to it" (Hogan, 1997, p. 32). But where this happens not to be so, as in the case of pre-independent India, citizens can individually and collectively command the moral authority to resist. As Locke would write, "Men being by nature, all free, equal and independent, no one can be put out of his estate, and subjected to the political power of another, without his consent" (Locke, 1963, pp. 374–375; Hogan, 1997, p. 32). While "the struggle over the nature and extent of citizenship has itself been a central medium of social conflict[,] it has also provided a means through which various classes, groups and movements seek to enhance and protect their rights and opportunities—rights in terms of legitimate spheres of independent action" (Held, 1989, p. 200).

The Problem of Stateness

The state is never a panacea for all of mankind's problems; rather, it offers an institutional basis in the search for new and practical solutions. "Things and men form the environment for each of man's activities; yet this environment, the world into which we are born, would not exist without the human activity which produced it" (Arendt, 1958, p. 22). While human actions are rarely imagined outside the confines of the state, but where such is the case, the state becomes the oppressor or the victim. For much of Gandhi's pre-Independence struggles, the state (in its colonial garb) was the oppressor, but it took the resilience of forces from the outside to collapse the internal institutions and, above all, the moral legitimacy to maintain its *stateness*. While it can be a force for good, the state also harbors an intrinsic paradox: the ability to exercise justice as well as injustice and an uncanny ability to seek its own survival above and beyond that of its constituent elements (citizens).

Invariably, what makes the state are simply the individuals who are engaged in various activities within the context of existing institutions, laws, rules and regulations, and also the prevailing social norms and traditions. Because there is no other *state* outside of this configuration; we can always say that the problem of the state is generally a human problem. It is a problem borne of the tension inherent in the series of relationships that emerge in the process of carrying out the various activities needed to sustain the state. Equally, it is the fabricated existence of the state that inspires many of the actions we take, even though the instrumentality of such actions are often measured by the distributive dividends and freedoms that accrue to us individually or collectively. Hence at the center of all state action there is always a human, and by changing the human state of mind, one can invariably change the nature of the state. "In many circumstances, the status of citizenship is not granted automatically; it must be fought for, as is exemplified by the many emancipatory movements of the 19th and 20th centuries" (Crossley, 2001, p. 34), such as the anticolonial movements, the struggles for independence and self-determination, the civil rights movements of the 1960s and the worldwide campaigns for group recognition, freedom, and respect. And like Gandhi, this is what citizenship-in-action embodies.

Notes

1 Sourced from http://www.indianchild.com/mahatma_gandhi.htm. Also http://history1900s.about.com/od/people/a/gandhi.htm?p=1.
2 http://www.indianchild.com/mahatma_gandhi.htm.

6 Citizenship as Culture

The Individual and the Public

Citizenship is not an eternal essence but a cultural artifact;
and like language, it depends on and changes with usage.

(van Gunsteren, 1998, p. 11)

The *public* has no independent essence apart from the individuals that constitute it; hence, it is only reflective of the presence of multiple others. But that, in itself, is a gross simplification of the construct. That is so because the *public* can be expressed in multiple ways, through the actions of individuals or through associational memberships of one kind or the other. In the context of the public, the individual disappears and is reduced to the form of an object expressed in the context of a group. The public exists, not as a *thing out there* but often as a consciousness in the minds of those who embody as well as think about it. We know about the public through the collective action or sentiments of individuals who participate in certain acts or events or who collectively express specific opinions on particular issues. Hence, the inclination "to adopt the same opinion as the public is nothing but a deceptive consolation, because the public is only there in abstraction" (Kierkegaard, 1946, p. 266).

Because the *public* lives in the minds of individuals as an imagined consciousness, a removal of the individual simultaneously negates any essence of the public. I prefer not to attribute the word "existence" to the public, since that would be conferring on it a double advantage. The individuals that constitute the public already exist, and it is through them that any idea of a public can assume essence as individuals reflect on it. As the Danish philosopher Soren Kierkegaard argues in *The Present Age*, it is "the real moment in time and the real situation of being simultaneous with real people, each of whom is something—that is what helps to sustain the individual; but the existence of a public produces neither a situation nor simultaneity" (Kierkegaard, 1946, p. 265). For Kierkegaard, the public is neither a nation nor a generation, a community or a society, or these particular men, for all these are only what they are through the concrete. Hence a "public is everything and nothing, the most dangerous of all powers and the most insignificant—and even when one can speak of a whole nation in the name of the public, but still the public will be less than a single real man, however unimportant" (Kierkegaard, 1946, p. 267). It is often said that public approval of a policy grants it greater legitimacy, but it still begs the question as to what extent such a policy is correlated with the ideal of legitimacy and its measurement.

The irony of the public is that it has a dual quality that is both constitutive and mutually exclusive. In the same way that individual consciousness constitutes the public, the public also reflects a negation of the same individual consciousness that made it possible. When we supplant individual opinions in place of public opinion, we create a sense of denial and the tendency for people "to feel one's reality as reflected in something external to oneself—in some collective organization" (Kierkegaard, 1946, p. 260). This condition is akin to what Karl Jaspers (1932) refers to as the deluding snares of external demand that undermine the existential resolve for man to be truly himself. The individual therefore sees himself as a reflection of a reified consciousness, of which he was instrumental in the formation but through which he has also lost the freedom to be himself and to act unhindered on his own behalf. The "self as conceived in the mainstream literature identifies an autonomous self-aware real person; but in the public, that real person might not be self-aware or fully autonomous" (Sementelli, 2009, p. 54). For it is only "from the standpoint of the self-conscious being, social practices and institutions appear as the embodiment of norms, standing in need of justification to him if he is to voluntarily acquiesce in them" (Gauthier, 1992, p. 157).

The Self as Objectified Reality

Lost amid the abstraction conceived as the public, the ensuing dynamic emerges as a result of tension generated out of the conflict between two competing identities—a reluctant obedience to *groupness* and the quest for *self-affirmation* or reclamation. Considered in its ordinary nature, each and every individual is an existential project that requires continued affirmation and generation of will for its validation—a will to affirm, to reject and to initiate action. It is by what you say or do that we have an essence of your particular being and that which distinguishes you from the rest of us. To the extent that the individual and the concept of the public are joint developments, in Foucauldian terms, the individual is simply a docile and mute body or more specifically a "mute solidity" (Dreyfus and Rabinow, 1983, p. 143). In this regard, individual identities as understood are simply expressions of *will-in-action*, codified and rested in the cognition of the *others*—in that collective consciousness that passes for the public.

In various ways, the crystallized consciousness of the public reflects *social facts*—"which exist only in the individual consciousness and through it" (Durkheim, 1994, p. 434). Social facts consist of relevant laws, norms and social conventions that shape individual action—"his ways of acting, thinking, and feeling, and though external to the individual, are endowed with power of coercion of which they control him" (Durkheim, 1994, p. 434). When individuals act in support of the public, such action also helps to recreate the same condition under which independent action and freedom are denied. The power that generates the impulse to conform does not come from within but from without and is premised on a common interpretation of social meanings by individuals. Such interpretation "involves clarifying the field of concepts that constitute a social practice and provides for shared values and sense of community" (Martin, 1994, p. 258). This is so because one cannot turn back upon oneself, thus becoming self-conscious, other than by imaginatively assuming the perspective of the other through the public (Mead, 1967). For Mead (1967) the self-dialogical process is constitutive of reflective thought and decision making because it explains how selfhood can both integrate an individual into a community, affording him or her a sense of belonging, and also give rise to reflective and argumentative agency (Crossley, 2001, p. 36).

Kierkegaard and others might see any semblance of the public as fraudulent and deceitful. It may be the "case that in abandoning oneself to it, one does not feel the pressure it exerts; but once we try to oppose its collective manifestation, it is only then that we come to the realization that we have become victims of having ourselves created that which actually forced itself from without" (Durkheim, 1994, p. 435). Because it impressed itself on us not necessarily by force but through repeated obedience to the collective consciousness of the public, it thus becomes a guiding norm for individual action and reasoning in particular subject matters. In the sense that "normative components are part of a cultural system that also transcends the individual" (Parsons, 1977, p. 161), "all culture is a matter of normative control or the guidance of action" (Parsons, 1977, p. 169).

The Individual Moment

Traditionally, the idea of citizenship connotes two main characteristics: legal status and a normative conception of social membership, substantive equality and inclusion (Marshall, 1950). While Aristotle's account lies in an instrumental conception of citizenship (1962), he qualifies it as an entitlement (not as an absolute right) that can only be earned *in lieu* of service to the community. By making the community (or state) the central element in any validation of citizenship, Aristotle argues that only 'good' states make for good citizens.

It should include "their sense of identity and how they view potentially competing forms of identities; a common desire to participate in the community process in order to promote the public good; and their willingness to show self-restraint and exercise personal responsibility in choices which affect their health, environment, and the wider community" (Kymlicka and Norman, 1994, p. 353).

Seen in this light, citizenship can thus be construed as a habit, a behavior and an attitude which when collectively expressed by members of the community helps to secure the public good. When this habit acquires enduring value and becomes embedded in the very idealism that drives individual and collective action, shared ownership in the project of the community becomes possible.

While the traditional conception of citizenship is limited to its interpretation as a nominal term tied to the membership of a community, I also see citizenship as a dynamic construct that should be viewed as a process through which specific rights and obligations are exercised. In other words, what ought to matter is a form of *citizenship-in-action* drawn upon *citizenship-as-norm* but set apart from the very actions and obligations that must be validated as both truth and possibility. Because citizenship in this regard is connected to a communally held value premise, it thus becomes, in and of itself, an *ordering device* that defines the scope and boundaries of what is or is not permissible in the larger community. Hence, as long as people abide by responsible and acceptable conduct in the exercise of their daily activities, they in turn validate the principles that undergird their collective notion of citizenship.

Hence, as the rise of group-based claims further erodes the sense of shared civic purpose and solidarity within contemporary society, the prospects of recovering traditional forms of identity and *citizenship-in-action* in our contemporary experience became more elusive.

Citizenship as Culture and Ideology

While it is structurally anchored on the state system, the central value of citizenship lies in the practical role it plays in the service of community in terms of welfare, security and cultural harmony. In all human societies, cultures emerge from people's struggles to manage uncertainties and create some degree of order in social life. In this context, cultures provide people with accepted ways of expressing and affirming their beliefs, values and norms and by providing them with procedural repertoires or forms that members of a community use to express the substance as well as make sense of their respective worlds (Trice and Beyer, 1993). Cultural forms imbue actions and other activities with meanings; they enable people to communicate and celebrate their ideas in many different ways. "The role of ideas in shaping behavior has a long intellectual pedigree, and during the 19th century was largely coded under the concept 'ideology'" (Scott, 2014, p. 150). As a collective phenomenon, our cultural responses to daily experiences falls into two categories: *ideologies*—shared, emotionally charged belief systems; and *forms*—observable entities, including actions through which members of a community express, affirm and communicate the substance of their culture to one another.

Cultures cannot be produced by individuals acting alone; rather, they originate and endure as individuals interact with one another. "It is structured in terms of patternings of meaning which, when stable, imply in turn generalized complexes of constitutive symbolisms that give an action system its primary sense of direction, and which must be treated as independent of any particular system of social interaction" (Parsons, 1977, p. 178). Belonging to a culture involves believing what others believe and doing as they do. In turbulent times, culture helps a people to manage their anxieties and disagreements and to channel their individual emotions and resistance in such a way that it does not fundamentally undermine the socially established order for achieving deliberative consensus. Though it may seem inherently symbolic, cultures are historically based; hence, a particular culture will be based in the unique history of a particular group of people coping with a unique set of physical, social, political and economic circumstances. Once individuals in a cultural group come to share some set of beliefs, ideas and practices, these eventually take on a life of their own, thus creating "the possibilities of their preservation over time, and of their diffusion from one personality or social system into another" (Parsons, 1977, p. 178).

But while cultures create continuity and persist across generations of members, they are not static, but dynamic. Cultures continually change and adapt, more or less as a result of changes in the larger political and social environment. Externally induced cultural changes are often subtle and incremental, while internally driven cultural changes are dramatic and radical. Because a dramatic shift away from the *status quo* is more likely to be noticed, it often generates increased and emotion-laden resistance. Because enduring cultures allow for the creation of a stable social order, continuity, collective identity, commitment and the management of uncertainties, they have enduring value in the exercise and practice of citizenship. Because they provide causal models for explaining and legitimating collective and individual behaviors, cultures are also ideologies. Hence, to the extent that ideologies explain and justify existing social systems in ways that make them seem natural, logically compelling, and morally acceptable; cultures that endure require honorable and committed citizens to be moral agents in the pursuit of the community interest.

Culture as Institution

In the American context, culture transcends a lot of varied history. It transcends many symbols of the national heritage and world view: the communitarian ideals of interdependent individualism, the rustic competitive spirit of western frontier adventurism, the extended ethno-linguistic system that has remained the locus of economic activity and identification, and a liberated market economy founded on the laissez-faire model. However, my concept of institutions goes beyond what could be found in the contemporary interpretation. I generally include ordinary and routine individual behaviors repeated over time in such a way that they fit nicely into the prevailing social convention. The law is an institution, but it would require individuals to obey it. To the extent the law ends up shaping an individual's behavior in such a way that he or she conforms to an acceptable social convention, the very act of obedience, when exercised over time takes on a life of its own. To the extent that such laws serve as an *ordering device* in situations of this nature, it thus becomes a regulatory institution.

While institutions help to maintain consistency and predictability in the behavior of community or social actors, even when performance fails to meet expectations, institutions provide a natural basis in the search for new solutions. In the same way that institutions enhance democratic compromise, they also mitigate the chances of personalizing cultural issues into political conflicts. Hence, "a major activity of institutions is educating individuals into knowledgeable citizens" (March and Olsen, 1989, p. 161). A knowledgeable citizen is one who is familiar with the rules of appropriate behavior and the moral and intellectual virtues of the community and who thus knows the institutional reasons for behaviors and can justify them by reference to the requirements of a larger order (MacIntyre, 1988). Institutional durability and legitimacy are enhanced as an institution is integrated into the larger social order in such a way that changes in one institution necessitate reciprocal changes in others. Because institutions embody "social patterns that, when chronically reproduced, owe their survival to relatively self-activating social processes" (Jepperson, 1991, p. 145), the average citizen must thus come to accept the necessity and importance of critical institutions.

Though collective action dilemmas generally lead to the creation of institutions to solve them, institutions provide the means by which cooperation dividends are captured and sustained. By shaping change to make it more consistent with existing procedures and practices, institutions maintain stability in the face of pressure to change. Institutions provide integrative norms and sanctions that affect the ways individuals and groups become activated within and outside established rules of appropriate behavior; the level of trust among citizens and leaders, common aspirations, belief systems, traditions and norms of a political community, and the rules that govern the existence of these institutions. In neglecting the language of culture and tradition that speaks to everyday imagination, the most energetic of languages—to the extent that it forms part of the fabric of citizenship—becomes endangered.

Culture as Social Capital

Because shared culture has a socially binding quality, it can help to bridge philosophical and idiosyncratic differences among community members. A critical fact that has wrecked many communities has been the lack of a unifying and facilitative social culture, deep communal cleavages, lack of mutual trust, and opportunistic tendencies based on absolute self-interest. Deep communal cleavages have a tendency to complicate or even undermine the give-and-take necessary for mutual accommodation. Social capital is defined as features of social life-networks, norms and trust that enable participants to act together more effectively to pursue shared objectives. To the extent that the norms, networks and trust link substantial sectors of the community and 'bridge' differences and underlying social cleavages, then the enhanced cooperation is likely to serve the broader interests and be widely accepted (Putnam, 1995b).

Social capital is viewed as the internal social and cultural coherence of society, the norms and values that govern interactions among people and the institutions under which they live; hence it is the glue that holds societies together, without which there can be no progress or human well-being. It refers to our relations with one another, and the more we connect with other people, the more we trust them, and vice versa. The concept of social capital is also consistent with the virtues of democracy. In practice, democracy requires a sense of affinity between the citizens to surpass other loyalties. Because this is lacking in many countries and communities, deep-seated cleavages developed along parochial lines have the tendency to create an increasingly intransigent social culture where compromises and accommodation between and within groups are almost impossible to attain.

The 'Public' in Public Service: Embracing Moral Agency

The contemporary practice of public administration is in flux as reflected in changing values and management philosophies, all of which stand to affect the way we do government business as well as the delivery of public services. Structurally, there is now a continuous blurring of the boundaries among government, private and non-profit sectors and increasing mobility or sector-switching among employees and employers; this, invariably, has given public service a broader meaning within a multi-sectoral component (Bowman et al., 2004, p. 6; Light, 1999, pp. 127–128). These new challenges would require "new administrative strategies that cross national boundaries, support rapid decision making in a world of twenty-four-hour markets and media, embrace multidisciplinary knowledge-building, and support prevailing institutional norms and legitimacy" (Durant, 2006, p. 180). Consequently, "the dynamic external and internal environment creates the need for professional managers who possess technical, ethical, and leadership competencies to meet the complex governance challenges of the twenty-first century" (Bowman et al., 2004, p. 5).

Due to the simple fact that many public sector problems are not discrete or technical demanding straightforward answers or solutions (Bowman et al., 2004, p. 7), they are problems that oftentimes reflect a complex mix of enigma, riddles, and esotericism—much of which we have come to know as "wicked problems." Finding solutions to "wicked problems" is like trying to catch water as it is continuously poured into a woven basket. Public administrators must therefore seek first to define the parameters and the relativity of the "wicked problems" that confront them and then devise innovative approaches (coping mechanisms) to bring them to manageable levels. There is also a requirement for the development of individual moral agency. The idea of a free moral agent is limited to those exercises of rights that do not infringe on the rights of others, hence individual action is a restricted form of free expression confined and limited by the prevailing social and political conventions as well as the boundaries of the law.

Public servants must, therefore, "develop the administrative rationality and an ingrained disposition to recognize the extent to which 'wicked problems' can constrain resources as well as influence resource-based accountability requirements" (Durant, 2006, p. 195). There are two sets of rationality: objective rationality, based on the law as well as the nature of organizational relationships, rules and procedures, and subjective rationality—how administrators exercise judgement and discretion. But whatever template is used to "make publicly relevant decisions must be seen to be moral and absolute, as well as reflect both the symbolic and real authoritative allocation of values in society" (Bowman et al., 2004, p. 7). Nonetheless, it is not inconceivable to argue that the consummate professional administrator must go beyond mastery of specific technical competencies, but must also embrace sound political and moral judgment in carrying out official duties and exercising administrative discretion. This later point is made much more difficult and poignant because "American democratic traditions reflect a tension between *political* and *professional* control of the public service" (Bowman et al., 2004, p. 16).

Administrative Competencies and Organizational Renewal

In their work titled *The Professional Edge: Competencies in Public Service*, James Bowman and his colleagues (Bowman et al., 2004) delineate three sets of competencies that are critical in the new public service, vis: *technical, ethical and leadership* competencies. I will illustrate below and draw upon their three categories, but I will also add a fourth category, which I call *communicative competency*—to make it more complete as well as realistic in the emerging administrative lay of the land.

Technical Competency

According to Bowman et al. (2004, p. 22), competence in one's chosen field and practice is an essential element of professionalism. There is a need to acquire mastery of basic planning methods—*strategic planning* and work-force planning, effective *program management* and *resource stewardship*—in an era of increasing fiscal stress and today's results-oriented environment. All these would require four skill sets (Bowman et al., 2004, p. 22):

- Job task mastery: to update and correct for existing or recurrent skills set deficiencies; career development opportunities.
- Project management: developing abilities in organization, planning, scheduling, budgeting, risk management, technical reviews and audit evaluation.
- Information technology skills: ability for people to work together and to exchange information in distant locations as well as engage in virtual interactions.
- Productivity improvement: ability to engage in quality management, process reengineering, and performance measurement.

Ethical Competency

The second point of the skills triangle refers to ethical capacity. To cope with the changes in the external and internal environment, public servants need to buttress technical skills with ethical competencies, such as *moral reasoning, values management and prudent decision-making* (Bowman et al., 2004, p. 26). Accordingly, the first is to "reinforce public confidence in the public service by ensuring that those delivering services—inside or outside of government—are in compliance with professional best practices; and secondly, adhering to high standards of conduct, minimizing partisanship, avoiding scandals, spending money wisely, and being responsive to citizens' needs" (Bowman et al., 2004, p. 26). Four sets of abilities are needed (Bowman et al., 2004, p. 26):

- Principled moral reasoning
- Recognition of ethics-related conflicts
- Refusal to do something unethical
- Always doing the right things (possibly consistent with existing ethical theory or universal moral principles).

Leadership Competency

The third point in the competency triangle is leadership skills. "The shift in the environment of public service from hierarchical, bureaucratic, government-run programs to 'networks' of goods and service providers from public, private, and nonprofit sectors demonstrate the need for new forms of leadership" (Bowman et al., 2004, p. 30; See Kalu, *Managing People and Information in Complex Organizations*, 2008). "Top down, command-and-control styles, while not necessarily a thing of the past, are gradually giving way to *collaborative* approaches to shared leadership; hence leaders need skills in *assessment, negotiation, and change management*" (Bowman et al., 2004, p. 30).

Because the hierarchical organization is slowly disappearing or, at best reorganizing, the top-down mechanism of control must now embrace new methodologies in which leaders would be expected to properly "be mindful of amassing facts, articulating goals, working effectively with a range of stakeholders, inspiring trust, cajoling, and embracing public involvement" (Bowman et al., 2004, p. 31). "Effective administrative leadership would require an ability to connect with the persons affected by administration and the larger pool of existing and potential stakeholders" (Durant, 2006, p. 193), and "it has been shown that citizens' opinion of bureaucracy improves when public administration is seen up close rather than considered abstractly" (Goodsell, 2015, p. 76).

Communicative Competency

The mainstream focus on the desirability of citizenship and civic engagement consistently embrace discussions of legitimacy, access and communication (Sementelli, 2009, p. 50). Because "every output of communication involves crossing a boundary, as does its receipt as input" (Parsons, 1977, p. 173), communicative competency revolves around how administrators are able to address their messages to relevant publics in such a way that the information does not become the problem, while avoiding conjectures that may undermine communication fidelity in substance and understanding of the information as conveyed. The speed with which mundane administrative statements take on a life of their own and become the issue has increased in recent years. In contrast to the current restrictive relationships within the bureaucracy as political appointees, can the average bureaucrat be bold enough to 'speak truth to power' and still get to keep his or her job? To what extent do these kinds of restrictions serve to limit the individual administrator's recognition of and contribution to the process of governing?

To the extent that asymmetrical communication patterns may lead to distortions, rational administrative action can only occur by removing restrictions on communication, including restrictions that preclude attempts to arrive at a consensus on important deliberations in the public sphere (Denhardt, 2011, p. 170). Jurgen Habermas (1979, pp. 118–119) argues that there is a need for "publicly, unrestricted discussion and communication; and that such communication at all levels of political and repoliticized decision-making processes is the only medium in which anything like 'rationalization' is possible." The contemporary administrator would need to acquire what Habermas calls *reflective-strategic* and *argumentative* capabilities (competencies), "not because strategic action or public discourse as such are the normal forms of interaction, but because communicative action involves the context-dependent employment of means of indirect understanding" (McCarthy, 1996, p. 350).

Therefore "moral consciousness and reciprocity result in the ability to employ interactive (communicative) competence for the conscious resolution of morally relevant conflicts" (McCarthy, 1996, p. 350). While it is understood that reciprocity may not be a fundamental norm of all interactions, Habermas argues that, at least, all subjects engaged in discourse have an intuitive grasp of reciprocity since it, invariably, belongs to the nature of interaction. Hence participants can draw upon this intuitive knowledge for the conscious resolution of moral questions. In the end, administrative leaders will spend more of their time managing information, meaning and content, as well as perception. Their changing roles will involve adaptation and innovation as a means of addressing the competing challenges of organizational work and professional ethics.

Acquiring technical competency helps to ensure that things are done correctly, while ethical competency leads to a more judicious application of the law and rules of the game, including the propensity to do the right things. Leadership competency is needed to provide direction as well as harness the energies of disparate service providers and orchestrate their efforts to advance the public interest; communicative competency is needed to address specific 'wicked problems' that may arise in the process of engagement with stakeholders and the general public. How you communicate the message and the multiple alternate readings (sense making) that go into it will go a long way to determine whether critical administrative decisions receive the broad support they need or whether such messages are drowned in the ideological divisions that characterize most public debate regarding critical issues of contemporary administrative and political governance.

7 Citizenship, Administrative Responsibility and Participation in Governance

One More Look

Despite the increased attention given to citizen participation by the federal government through a number of dramatic new social programs, the existing work in the field reflects a good many uncertainties about the phenomenon, the difficulty in coming to terms with its implications and the absence of criteria by which to measure its effectiveness and overall worth (Spiegel and Mittenthal, 1968, p. 3). In many contemporary writings in public administration (Denhardt, 1999; Gawthrop, 1998; Vigoda, 2002; Holzer, 1999; Kirlin and Kirlin, 2002), we are confronted by the continued call for citizen participation and engagement in government as if that is an end in itself rather than a means to an end. "While there is something very seductive about the idea that people ought to be directly involved in the decisions that affect their lives; the gap between our ideal and its practice appears to have energized us rather than deterred us" (Roberts, 2004, p. 341). "Despite the warnings of its dangers, limitations, impracticality, and expense, especially in large, complex, heterogeneous, technologically advanced twenty-first century societies, it still remains an ideal that animates many of our theories and beliefs" (Roberts, 2004, p. 341).

But in a fundamental way, the seeming hysteria for citizen participation seems misplaced because it tends to mask the fact that as a reflection of our representative democracy, citizens are already participating in government through their elected representatives. Ours is not a direct democracy, rather what we have is a representative democracy in which citizens elect their representatives and hold them accountable through elections. By participating in the electoral system, paying taxes and obeying the law and social conventions, citizens are already engaged in the art of political and administrative governance. Hence the rising clamor, both in scholarly literature and in academic discourse, has seemed to redefine the traditional role of citizenship in a representative democracy as well as how best to govern the administrative state.

On the other hand, such a clamor for increased citizen participation can also be construed as a reflection of a growing vote of 'no confidence' and public cynicism driven by what most people see as the continued insularity and politicization of the bureaucratic system. Suffice it then to say that citizens do not necessarily seek direct participation in governance; rather they want representation and accountability. The reason is that citizens are already participating through the electoral process, recall petitions, public opinion polls, public hearings, advisory boards, citizen commissions, community task forces, protests and making complaints to public agencies, calls to offices of congresspersons, litigation in the courts and expressions of free speech rights.

Furthermore, and based on the premise of normative democratic theory, one can argue that citizen participation reinforces the pluralistic nature of liberal democracy. It has been argued that "with citizen participation, formulated policies might be more realistically grounded in citizen preferences, and the improved support from the public might create a less divisive, combative populace to govern and regulate" (Irvin and Stansbury, 2004, p. 55). Equally, the general euphoria surrounding the virtues of (direct) citizen participation in governance (as if it is some new invention) could be seen as an attempt to arbitrarily bridge the division of labor between what appointed bureaucrats and elected representatives are supposed to do and what citizens as legitimate benefactors of good governance are supposed to expect from those who (ought to) serve them. Citizen participation in governance absent of the traditional roles indicated above challenges the essential notions of representative democracy, administrative accountability and political division of labor.

To clarify these distinctions and their emerging challenges, this chapter aims to discuss competing issues of representative democracy and administrative responsibility, citizen participation in decision making and the problem of reconciling administrative and political values in governance. The concluding section will draw on a review of citizen opinions and preferences on critical aspects of political participation, personal satisfaction and efficacy in policy outcomes. This will be based on the ICPSR "*American Citizen Participation Study, 1990*," conducted by Sidney Verba et al. and obtained through the Inter-University Consortium for Political and Social Research.

Representative Democracy and Administrative Responsibility

The idea of representative democracy was driven home to the Founding Fathers of the American state, in part through the writings of John Locke and a simple belief that a form of governance in which the masses played a direct role in decision making concerning the affairs of the state would amount to a 'rule of the rabble.' It was a tacit recognition of the inherent virtues of a social order in which only the most endowed few, not necessarily in the mold of Plato's ruler class, but with a unique intelligence, would be able to decide in the best interest of all. Their vision was a form of limited government in which ultimate power rested with the citizens through the electoral mandate, while a series of institutional 'checks and balances' would checkmate the individual and collective excesses of those who have been elected to govern. However, the problem of representative democracy rests not in the fact that it does not afford direct citizen participation in governance, but rather that it offers citizens a means of securing political accountability devoid of the requisite administrative responsibility.

While citizens can have the opportunity to vote for or against a candidate running for public office, they do not have such opportunity when it comes to bureaucrats who hold much of the decision-making authority in administrative governance.

Because bureaucrats are 'appointed' and therefore directly accountable to the executive, the idea of indirect accountability to the public can only be made possible through the political filters of the President or executive branch. Such indirect accountability cannot be construed as value-neutral, especially in a state where divergent views on the nature and scope of public policy are accepted as routine. The irony, though, is that "the public sector and civil service (bureaucracy) do not exist in their own right as embodiments of the wider political community but must be legitimized through how efficient they are in delivering service to the people; hence the election channel remains a slow and ineffective way of influencing the civil service" (Aberbach and Christensen, 2003, p. 503) or holding it accountable.

Where Bureaucrats Have Won

There is the general belief that because "most politicians mess things up, it is therefore preferable to leave it to independent bodies (public agencies) to make decisions about regulation and about what public policies are implemented" (Aberbach and Christensen, 2003, p. 501). But when those decisions go wrong or when citizens seem not to be so impressed about the outcome of government policy, 'politicians' suffer the public opprobrium while bureaucrats or administrative leaders incur passive accountability. The generally insular nature of bureaucratic life and the absence of direct public accountability through either elections or some kind of oversight protect administrative leaders from the same kind of public scrutiny leveled at politicians.

To secure increased legitimacy for their actions, administrative leaders have generally been receptive to the idea of citizen participation or engagement in governance through public meetings, focus groups, opinion surveys, and other channels of public input into the decision-making process. The irony is that on the one hand such a call represents an implicit admission that something is wrong with the way administration is conducted, and on the other hand, it tends to reinforce a pessimistic view of bureaucracy's impact on its clients (the citizens) and perhaps, "an image of public servants as untrustworthy and bumbling, entangled in red tape, and failing to apply the common sense with which average citizens are endowed" (Holzer, 1999, p. 5).

But to the extent that the role of the citizen is limited to the decision-making process, it becomes an issue as to who would be responsible for the effects or outcome of a policy. Would it therefore be the citizens (who contributed in the decision making), or would it be the administrative officials who implemented the policy? If so, how much responsibility should each party bear for the policy outcome?

This dilemma was also aptly expressed in Kakabadse, Kakabadse and Kouzmin (2003, p. 45) pointing to "the necessity of not allowing the role of elected representatives to be undermined by splitting responsibilities from accountabilities; and thoroughly utilizing means that give society greater access to the implementation of policy while maintaining elected representatives who are accountable for outcomes." These have nonetheless remained major concerns whenever the issue of citizen participation comes up. First, they dilute the onus of administrative responsibility and second offer, by default, a seemingly innocent avenue for legitimizing potential administrative incompetency. Two factors explain this: a postmodern misconception of the ideal behind citizen participation and a philosophical dichotomy between political (public) and administrative (bureaucratic) values. I will present the thrust of my argument by drawing from the classic thesis of Aristotelian republican ethics as well as explicate the basic limiting factors of citizen participation in the context of a liberal representative democracy.

Citizen Participation in Decision Making: How Effective?

There has been a lingering ambiguity as to what is the end of citizen participation in governance (Fagence, 1977; Davis, 1972; Almond and Verba, 1963; Calhoun, 1971; Downs, 1967; Olson, 1996; London, 1994; Adonis and Mulgan, 1994; Denhardt, 1999; Gawthrop, 1998; Vigoda, 2002; Holzer, 1999; Kirlin and Kirlin, 2002). Some have argued that "low levels of popular (citizen) participation in political decision making are *de facto* expressions of a preference for non-involvement; others suggest that modern institutional structures frustrate attempts by citizens to become involved in the decision process; and yet others hold the view that participation by the 'masses' would be debilitating to political systems" (Fagence, 1977, p. 21). Hence, this "lack of consensus affords more opportunity for indulgence in the charismatic appeal of the term and its expressions" (Fagence, 1977, p. 22).

But for whatever view one holds, the underlying argument suggests that popular citizen participation is the most 'acceptable' route to encouraging participatory democracy in the hope of making government more directly accountable to the public interest. To the extent that "broad participation does not necessarily assure representative participation" (Weeks, 2000, p. 360); hence, to practice both types of democracy within a single system of governance essentially negates the structural differences that make them mutually exclusive. The key paradox this creates is how to reconcile the functional basis of liberal *representative democracy* with direct *participatory democracy* in the process of holding government more accountable.

Political Participation and the Polis

It was through the great works of Plato (*The Republic*) and Aristotle (*Politics*) that we came to learn more about the nature of political morality that existed in ancient Athens as well as many other Greek city-states. Contrary to the widely held view among the Greeks that democracy safeguarded the equal rights of every citizen to participate in government, "there remained the recognition that full participation in every aspect of decision making was physically and managerially impossible, hence available energies and expertise should be distributed appropriately between various organs of government" (Fagence, 1977,

p. 24). While most Greek scholars and philosophers expressed doubts about both the philosophy and the practice of democracy, Plato and Aristotle were very unfavorable toward it, and both were equally opposed to the idea of absolute (or natural) equality in both nature and political society.

Although Plato believed that people ought to be involved in their own destiny, he found it unattainable since it pre-supposed a well-educated and informed public who would and could respond intelligently to this task. He pointed out that, since in the phenomenal world we do not find such people in the masses, we must rely on government by the enlightened elite—this being infinitely superior to the bungling of an ignorant and ill-informed multitude (Plato, 1871). "It is therefore of consequence to modern attempts to practice meaningful citizen participation in decision making in as much as the available record of classical democracy does not reveal an unequivocal egalitarian situation, and in fact, seems to render the current cultural experiment inappropriate for adoption in the present complex societal context without suitable translation and manipulation" (Fagence, 1977, p. 25).

The almost puritan model of citizen participation we seek in contemporary governance systems is very much at odds with the Aristotelian tradition and hence creates a contradiction that is fundamentally opposed to our liberal representative democracy. This is due essentially to the fact that Aristotle did not subscribe to an unqualified or pluralistic model of citizen participation (by the masses). His argument focuses on the instrumental aspects of citizenship and the officially sanctioned obligations that undergird it. Hence, in an Aristotelian republic, the criterion of citizenship is the extent of an individual's (officially sanctioned) participation in the community or state in such a way that it enhances the good life for all members of the community or *polis* (Kalu, 2003a, p. 420). The type of political participation Aristotle seeks is not a kind of unmitigated public access into the affairs of the government; rather he sees participation as an instrumental process that can be made efficacious only as long as it contributes to the general good of the *polis*. For him, it is the utility function (the end to which participation serves) that should matter, not necessarily the activity itself.

Contrary to the postmodern view of political participation, especially in polities that are governed under liberal democracies, the issue of citizen participation is viewed as a central ideal—a means that offers to citizens the opportunity for inclusiveness, a sense of belongingness, self-worth, and the fundamental right to be heard. More credence is given to the exercise itself as opposed to what the policy outcome would be. Hence citizen participation provides a means of extending the democratic franchise to people who would not otherwise have merited the 'officially sanctioned' authority to do so. It provides one more layer of legitimacy for governmental action.

In a recent study of the US Forest Service, Kathleen Halvorsen (2003, p. 541) concluded that while exposure to quality citizen participation explained a significant portion of participants' trust in government and tolerance of different viewpoints; "public managers on the other hand, were more interested in participation's role in shaping the legitimacy of specific decisions as well as participants' trust in their organization. They were interested in citizens' tolerance for those with differing views insofar as it affects their expectations of public agency decisions" (Halvorsen, 2003, p. 541). What this study points to is that the utility of citizen participation is not really about public accountability, rather it is a conduit for securing increased legitimacy for agency decisions, which may already have been made by the agency but presented to citizens for debate and discussion after the fact.

In addition, the public servant (bureaucrat) already has enough information about the merits of the issue in question and thus stands to reinforce or, in most cases, impose his or her professional or political judgment and understanding of the issue in such a way that it leaves little choice for the citizen to disagree but to consent. In most circumstances, the bureaucrat could overwhelm the deliberation with so much information overload and technical complexities that the average citizen would of necessity yield rather quickly to 'superior' knowledge. The degree of power distance between bureaucrat and citizen often makes citizen participation in governance substantively meaningless.

Civic Pluralism and Its Democratic Deficit

While citizen participation may reinforce specific values inherent in a democracy, it at the same time contradicts the fundamental principle of majoritarian politics. The issue is not about how many people may have contributed in shaping a particular policy premise, but rather the extent to which it reflects the broad social and political preferences of the larger society. The limitation thus is that the opinions of a few that were present at the deliberation would be passed off as a reflection of the views of the many that were absent. "Citizen voices are very unequal, not everyone votes; only small proportions of the citizenry work in campaigns or make contribution, or send letters or faxes to Washington, D.C." (Verba, 1996, p. 2). "But then only a small proportion of the public uses this means, and that minority is not a random sample of the population; but it comes disproportionately from the more advantaged members of society" (Verba and Nie, 1972; Verba, Scholzman and Brady, 1995). "Participation by a few citizens with a special interest in the subject matter offers policy makers a skewed representation of the views of the general public and, worse, conveys to citizens the impression of special interest domination of the policy agenda" (Weeks, 2000, p. 361). While the results may, in specific circumstances, reflect the policy preferences of a cross-section of the community, the larger goals of broader citizen participation as well as its credibility will have been sacrificed.

On the other hand, there is no guarantee that what was discussed in the deliberative exchange between bureaucrats and citizens would be implemented without going through the normal political filters that would safeguard the interest of public officials and their political clientele. While citizens may be able to contribute various viewpoints on important policy issues, they may still lose out on the very part where their viewpoints could have been able to make the crucial changes they desire. There is little doubt that the implementation stage offers bureaucrats the greatest opportunity to exercise discretion or independent judgment in the exercise of their public duties. In those circumstances where inputs from citizen participation would jeopardize long-entrenched bureaucratic culture and standard operation procedures, any conclusion on the administrative efficacy of citizen participation would certainly yield in favor of the status quo and the prevailing political environment. The criterion of 'citizen participation' could assist public bureaucrats to cut through the complex, multi-valued nature of domestic politics and improve their judgment of the relative importance of different objectives. However, this ideal unfortunately lends itself more readily to being used by administrative leaders "as political rhetoric for justifying their decisions and gaining support rather than as an exact, well-defined criterion that enables them to determine what actions and decisions to take" (George, 2005, p. 335).

To the extent that the desirability of the policy initiative and the feasibility of its implementation are muddled in the rhetoric of political language and power plays, the concept of 'policy legitimacy' becomes relevant and useful in this context. For the administrator or bureaucrat, the day-to-day actions he takes on behalf of specific policy initiatives (popular or unpopular) "becomes less vulnerable to the many pressures and constraints that various manifestations of 'democratic control' would otherwise impose on his ability to pursue that policy in a coherent and consistent manner" (George, 2005, p. 336).

It may be the case that if "citizen participants are misled into thinking that their decisions will be implemented, and then the decisions are ignored or merely taken under advisement, resentment will develop over time" (Irvin and Stansbury, 2004, p. 59). It therefore remains in doubt to what extent citizen participation advances substantive democracy as well as strengthens the character of political life. In all, "expecting administrators to be the prime movers in their own legitimation raises both a problematic normative question and a challenging empirical one" (O'Toole, 1990, p. 64). As Martin Rein (1969) puts it "involvement, although it facilitates legitimation, impedes innovation." It thus becomes a celebration of the *process* (normative democracy) as opposed to what desirable end it can provide (substantive democracy).

Social Structure and the Limits of Deliberative Consensus

Proponents of game theory and institutional models (North, 1990; Shepsle, 1989; Shepsle and Weingast, 1995; Brams, 1997; North and Weingast, 1989; Przeworski and Vreeland, 2002; Putnam, 1988; Mo, 1995; Smith, 1999; Tsebelis, 1995, 2002; Vaubel, 1986) are more likely to explain decision making as a subset of plots, strategies and zero-sum game, win-lose or win-win propositions. To them, every engagement is generally preceded by a series of rational calculations that ought to inform specific strategies in situations of increasing uncertainty and information asymmetry. Among some of the models used to encourage citizen participation in decision making and governance are town hall meetings, opinion surveys, voting, direct action, volunteerism, call-ins, petitions and referendums. Whatever form it takes, the common denominator in this process is that there is an exchange of information. While the primary aim is to achieve what I would call *deliberative consensus* among the parties involved, it is the structural relationship among the participants that determines whether there is a consensus or not or even when there is one, how meaningful and reflective it would be.

First, the average citizen comes to the deliberation with limited knowledge of the issues and the political-administrative philosophy that inform them. In addition, "the increased specialization and professionalization of pursuits within the arena of government has tended towards an elitist rather than a pluralist form of decision making" (Fagence, 1977, p. 331). Hence, citizens lack 'inside' knowledge of how most bureaucracies work, the internal challenges they face or the political imperatives they have to secure. On average, they have only a generic understanding of how government ought to function in the dynamic world of domestic and international politics. They suffer from information asymmetry. Limited information means that critical issues are not adequately (or democratically) deliberated upon; participation is superficial and decision making haphazard at best. "Certainly involving citizens in every decision raises important questions: how do you assure that an appropriate level of expertise is incorporated into the decision process? How can you be sure that the fullest and most complete knowledge is brought to bear on the problems of the state? And how can you incorporate the requirement of dialogue and deliberation that has always been considered an essential element of democracy?" (Denhardt, 1999, p. 2).

While the "essential condition of democracy is that all citizens have an equal opportunity to exert influence through political activity if they chose to do so; decisions are still controlled by the greatest number (majority) expressing their preferences in favor of a particular alternative" (Rosenbaum, 1978, p. 44). "As more government processes open up to citizen input, the need for citizen education and the need to provide citizens with the highest quality of information become more pronounced" (Simonsen and Robbins, 2000, p. 11). Hence, participation itself does not necessarily mean that every person's views or needs are reflected in the decision-making process, especially if you happen to be in the minority.

On the Social Psychology of Participation

The political utility of citizen participation should not be based only on how well it satisfies traditional democratic virtues; rather, we should focus on how the model of pluralism affects the way in which the political system distributes benefits among social groups and interests. Nonetheless, "it seems quite plausible to assume that particular structural features discourage some groups from participation because they limit their opportunities for success" (May, 1971, p. 19). Differences among individuals, both in their idiosyncrasies and perceptions, can present the greatest limiting factor for achieving a consensus on what is best for the citizenry. Ideological cleavages and partisan disagreements can also present filters through which individuals judge issues of relatively common interest.

"Besides most citizens lack sufficient political interest, knowledge, principle, and rationality" (May, 1971, p. 2), such that while some are able to develop the natural inclination for political involvement, others are more likely to become cynical and indifferent toward most issues of public concern.

For most people, participation is choice-driven, and the extent of their participation can depend on how they feel addressing a specific issue will make a difference in their lives. But the irony is that when those issues are not eventually addressed in the way people expect them to be addressed (even if unrealistic), they become frustrated, withdraw onto themselves, and are more likely not to participate in the future. Hence, we can rightfully state that citizen participation is a relative ideal that pertains only to those who have developed the habit, inclination and resources to become involved. Furthermore, it remains doubtful how persistent citizen commitment on an issue would be for the long term. We note that oftentimes an issue of high salience (for example the 9–11 terrorist attack in the US) can attract sustained civic engagement and public judgment, but over time direct interest seems to wane as most people either become complacent or indifferent to critical issues surrounding the original question.

Researches by Perry and Katula (2001) and Putnam (2002) have shown that positive attitudes about public affairs do not automatically equate to strong civic engagement, as measured by civic behaviors. As the gap between behavior and attitude widens, the reliance on citizen preferences becomes too ambiguous to provide much guidance for decision makers. This particular point becomes more obvious when considered in light of the fact that "citizen assessments arise less from direct and concrete experiences, but more or less, from abstract orientations (symbolic attitudes) that people have about government and politics" (Orr and West, 2007, pp. 649–650).

Political Versus Administrative Values: Whither the Difference?

The type of value system that shapes civic behavior in the political system is different from that which informs professional behavior in the administrative arena. While the former is political and the latter is administrative, suffice it then to say that "citizen participation occurs in the middle of the tension between politics and administration" (Simonsen and Robbins, 2000, p. 7). Woodrow Wilson's (1887) thesis on the politics-administration dichotomy reinforced the separateness of the administrative and political functions. While administration was to be guided by professional values and the principles of scientific management as was then evident in the private sector, political functions were meant to be guided by public consensus and deliberation that would in the final analysis reflect the will of the people. To the extent that citizen participation reflects a political activity, it also reinforces the classic tension between politics and administration.

In the process of citizen-agency exchange, all parties to the engagement operate from different sets of obligations, priorities and value premises. Robert

Seaver (1968, pp. 64–65) narrates a woeful tale of the political dynamics at work when citizens engage agencies in the process of civic participation. He points out that while: "The appointed administrator may be more or less sensitized to the web of interests surrounding the object of inquiry, and have greater of less skill in coping with it; yet he listens, but subordinates what he hears to what he has been told—or believes—is the most important objective." Other bureaucrats under him will fit what remains of the message into the iron maiden of procedures and programs at their disposal, and the technicians will further select what they are capable of responding to in light of their own professional disciplines and personal capacities. The result of this process may be a response that comes as a shock to the citizens who are unaware of the hazards of transmission loss and filtration that beset their original statements (Seaver, 1968, pp. 64–65).

Furthermore, "the bureaucrat or technician is frustrated at the citizen's apparent inability to understand that he cannot solve all problems because they are not all his responsibility; while on the other hand, the citizen is frustrated at the bureaucrat's apparent indifference to the richness and diversity of his wants and needs" (Seaver, 1968, p. 65). There are certain factors that influence whether individuals have or will develop the inclination for political or public involvement. "Individual traits as well as contextual factors influence participation levels; the issues and problems motivating participation are multidimensional by content and by objective" (Jennings, 1997, p. 362). Among these are differences in individual personality, ideological preferences, partisan beliefs, differences in individual sense making about political objects and symbols and the efficacy of specific policy alternatives in addressing issues of importance to them.

As the average citizen seeks for more openness and inquiry into the affairs of public bureaucracy, administrators naturally resort to defensive measures that limit the amount of information divulged in the process of the encounter. They oftentimes hide behind the mask of professional esotericism. In the end, "the inherent difficulty of some of the subject matter and the confusing way it is often presented by political (and administrative) leaders probably combine to discourage citizens from becoming more involved" (Sigel and Hoskin, 1981, p. 51). Hence, "the political nature of decision making and the inability to establish clear causal linkages in public policy domains may erode the importance" (Brown and Brudney, 2003, p. 32) of citizen participation as a model of inclusive (democratic) governance.

As Alexander George (2005, p. 354) points out, one of the characteristics of the US public is its impatience for quick results and its demand for frequent reassurances that a policy is succeeding. This impatience is often fed and exploited by the mass media (through public opinion polls) and by political opponents of the current administration's policy. "While the play of public opinion and politics can distort the difficult task of evaluating public policy; it can also erode its legitimacy, and can force changes in policy before it has had a chance to prove itself" (George, 2005, p. 354). The result of these domestic political factors is that they complicate the ability of the bureaucrat to pursue any long-range policy with the patience and professionalism that is needed.

Reconciling State and Citizenship: A Research Note

For Aristotle, "the political association which we call a state exists not simply for the purpose of living together but for the sake of noble actions" (1962, p. 121). Such noble actions are reflected in the collective obligation of every citizen to participate in the affairs of the *polis* (as long as such participation is officially sanctioned). Hence, the state itself can be secured by the individual actions of its citizens only to the extent that such actions contribute to the welfare of the community. However, this ideal negates the fact that in a representative democracy, the concept of a political community imposes a reciprocal obligation between the state and its citizens: The state offers protection, security and justice (public goods) to the citizens; citizens are expected to pay taxes, vote in elections, obey legal and social conventions and defend the state and its institutions.

But how do individual preferences connect to the actions of the state and its priorities? Do citizens feel that being involved in the affairs of the state would make any difference (a sense of political efficacy)? Do they see citizen participation as a function of their obligation to the state (legitimacy) or as a matter of discretionary choice (personal freedom)? By using data from the American Citizen Participation Study, 1990, developed by Sidney Verba et al., we can analyze specific citizen characteristics and responses that point to wide variations in how citizens view political participation as addressing issues of personal concern, political efficacy and inclusive democratic governance. While the study was designed to examine political and non-political civic participation in the United States, respondents were asked to comment on various topics, including their interest in politics and their party identification, voting status, campaign activities, electoral contributions and activity in community politics. Respondents also provided information about their own personal experiences with government programs, as well as their opinions on national and social problems and why people in the United States are not more active in politics.

In a study entitled *City Size and Civic Involvement in Metropolitan America*, J. Eric Oliver (2000) used the same 1990 data to analyze the effects of city size on participation in four local civic activities. Controlling for both individual and city-level characteristics, he found that people in larger cities are much less likely to contact public officials, attend community or organizational meetings or vote in local elections. While lower civic participation was attributed partly to differences in social relations and psychological orientation between residents of larger and smaller places, it was also discovered that people in big cities are less likely to be recruited for political activity by neighbors and are less interested in local affairs. The study thus suggests that structural characteristics such as level of urbanization, socioeconomic differences and residential patterns create differences in the kinds of issues that appeal to people as well as their level of interest to get involved in addressing civic problems.

Analysis and Discussion

The analysis here uses simple frequency distributions of citizen responses on 13 sets of questions based on the Verba et al. 1990 study. Comprising a total

Table 7.1 Frequency Distribution of Political Participation Acts

Measures of Participation	*%Yes*	*%No*
1. Made contributions to political candidates and parties	31.6	68.4
2. Written a letter to a public official	60.1	39.3
3. Gone to a meeting where you participated in making decisions	71.1	28.2
4. Contacted a government official	23.6	75.6
5. Made contributions to election campaigns and PACs	1.2	88.7
6. Felt Participation in protest made difference	16.2	33.5
7. Volunteered opinions about issues confronting your organization	47.7	52.3
8. Felt that local council would pay attention to my complaint	64.6	34.7
9. Contributed to public debate due to issues or problems	60.6	39.4
10. Voted in local community election	71.9	28.1
11. Voted in elections and found it exciting	14.1	63.4
12. Protested to influence government policy	81.1	7.9
13. Voted in elections to influence government	64.7	9.7

N = 2517 cases

sample of 2517 cases, the findings indicate the proportion of respondents who were engaged in several participatory activities or who felt that such activities were both exciting and politically efficacious. Table 7.1 provides the percentage responses from the sample. It shows that even though many of the respondents saw political participation as a way of influencing government, very few were able to make regular contacts with government officials. While most people voted in local community elections, they found the process of exercising this franchise to be quite laborious and not exciting. Perhaps this could be due to the contextual differences that exist between the act of voting and other forms of political participation. Voting in elections reflects an individual act carried out after much personal deliberation, while other forms of participation such as meetings, campaigns and protests more or less require collective deliberation and action.

In a similar vein, Table 7.2 provides citizens' responses regarding their reasons for participation or nonparticipation in various political activities. The frequency distributions indicate that a majority of the respondents felt that they lacked a general sense of political efficacy, did not think that the results of political participation would be worth the effort and were more concerned about personal as opposed to communal issues. Even though more people saw participation as a means to influence government (51.9%), 81.5% of the respondents did not feel that their participation would make any impact. What therefore could account for this level of disconnect between expectation and outcome? One explanation could be that most citizens do not see the kinds of changes they expect from participation, partly because of the insular nature of bureaucratic life as well as the political imperatives that shape administrative action.

Coupled with many other demands on their time, and the seemingly difficult task of penetrating the bureaucratic fortress, most citizens are reluctant to make follow-up inquiries as to the implementation results of agreed-upon policy objectives. That may be one reason there continues to be a consistent feeling of political

Table 7.2 Frequency Distribution of Reasons for Participation or Nonparticipation

Reasons for Participation	*%Yes*	*%No*
1. The chance to influence government policy	51.9	18.2
2. Duty as a citizen	53.4	14.7
3. Chance to make community or nation a better place to live	83.1	3.6
4. Wanted to learn about politics and government	18.2	55.7
5. The chance to further the goals of my party	30.5	39.1
6. I am the kind of person who does my share	26.6	24.8
7. I don't feel I can have an impact	14.7	81.5
8. Politics is too complicated to understand	51.2	45.2
9. I should take care of family before welfare of community	69.0	27.0
10. I don't have enough time for politics	65.5	30.6
11. Results of political participation not worth the effort	47.4	48.0
12. I find that politics can't help with family problems	46.8	49.3
13. Influence over national policy is little or nonexistent	78.6	21.3

N = 2517 cases

Table 7.3 Respondent's Sense of Political Efficacy: National Government Decision Making

Measure of Political Efficacy	*None*	*Little*	*Moderate*	*A lot*
How much do you believe you can influence NATIONAL government decisions?	30%	50%	18%	.02%

N = 2517 cases

Table 7.4 Respondent's Sense of Political Efficacy: Local Government Decision Making

Measure of Political Efficacy	*None*	*Little*	*Moderate*	*A lot*
How much do you believe you can influence LOCAL government decisions?	15%	33%	42%	10%

N = 2517 cases

inefficacy on the part of the respondents. As shown in Tables 7.3 and 7.4, the majority of the respondents were of the opinion that their participation would have very little or no influence on national and local government decision making. Participation can only be credible when citizens develop greater trust in government and a belief that it would be able to act in a manner that reflects agreed-upon policy choices as well as popular opinion.

Besides the issue of political efficacy, there are also other fundamental issues raised by the Verba et al. (1990) study. To what extent does the survey data accommodate differences in social structure and representation? Under what circumstances can the information be generalizable as well as reflective of broad-based policy decisions? Of the 2517 cases in the survey, the distribution along ethno-cultural lines was as follows: white (66%), black (19%), Asian (0.8%),

Alaskan Native (1.05) and Hispanic/Latino (11.6%). The survey also indicates that 89% of all those who made contacts to public officials (as part of political engagement) were white (90.4%), black (7.8%), and Hispanic (1.8%); the races of the public officials contacted were white (86%), black (9.8%) and Hispanic (3.5%).

What this points to is that while citizen participation may represent the broad interest and views of the majority, it does not provide a more democratic means for accommodating the broader interests of society. Furthermore, while the survey indicates level of education to be a crucial factor in citizen participation; it might mean that sections of society with low levels of education or many high school dropouts would less likely be involved in citizen participation activities. Hence, to encourage greater citizen participation might require government to develop policies that facilitate increased educational attainment and reduced high school dropouts among all sectors of society, especially minority populations.

Toward a Public Theory of Administrative Responsibility

It is "unquestionably true that American bureaucrats inhabit a particularly inhospitable landscape, and political campaigns of the past few decades have only contributed to the malaise they experience" (O'Toole, 1990, p. 63). But it is also equally true that the continued emphasis on citizen participation in governance "diminishes the institutional roles of government and ignores the central dimensions of citizenship that revolve around engagement as a means of judging what needs to be done, and in developing the civic skills necessary for effective persuasion and mobilization of resources to address collective issues" (Kirlin and Kirlin, 2002, p. 84). "How then will those to whom administrators are responsible—elected officials, the courts and citizens—know responsible public management when they see it?" (Bertelli and Lynn, 2003, p. 259).

In the contemporary administrative state, especially among liberal democracies, political responsibility can be secured through elections. The issue of securing administrative responsibility is somewhat problematic because bureaucrats are appointed and not elected. Hence much public opprobrium against bureaucracy is channeled indirectly through elected representatives in government, but elections have often time proven not to be the best means for making politicians more responsible and accountable.

We can require elected public officials or appointed bureaucrats (where necessary) to post quarterly reports of their policy making or administrative activities to a designated personnel clearinghouse (a variant of the General Accounting Office) that would authenticate such information before making it available for public access and scrutiny. In the same way that businesses provide quarterly reports of their earnings, this is perhaps one more approach the public sector could borrow from the private sector. This would allow the public to have more reliable information for evaluating the performance of elected officials beyond the usual rhetoric and spin of political action.

The same model can be expanded beyond what is currently available, to secure administrative responsibility by requiring more personnel and program evaluations of public agencies and their officials to be posted online. There is a need for increased transparency and public access to administrative and evaluation records that are ranked over a period of time for comparative purposes. When administrators recognize that their various actions or inactions face rigorous public scrutiny, they will be more disposed to behave in ways that serve the best interest of the citizens. With "widespread public benefit as the goal of any public policy process, it thus behooves the administrator to consider the advantages and disadvantages of the decision-making process when determining the most effective implementation strategy" (Irvin and Stansbury, 2004, p. 63). Accepting the fact that much or some of this is already being done in the public sector, it may need to be expanded beyond the record of roll calls, sponsorship of legislations or implementation of particularized or nonparticularized public policies. The ideal of citizen participation, while instrumental to broadening the scope of public input into the policy process, does not in itself imply that such policy decisions would be effective. From the perspective of the administrator, citizen participation serves more as a means of securing administrative legitimacy than administrative responsibility. To the extent that both cannot reasonably be construed as mutually exclusive, this is the irony of citizen participation.

8 Migration, Labor and Capital

Regulatory Challenges of Identity and Hybrid Communities

There are many issues that face the world of the twenty-first century. Among these are environmental problems, nuclear proliferation, terrorism, hunger, poverty, war and famine. Yet few of these pose as great a challenge to the state and its traditional identity than the issue of transnational immigration. While it can be acknowledged that transnational immigration has been encouraged by increasing and cheaper modes of transportation, communications and commerce, it may offer enormous prospects but at the same time portends serious consequences. The most critical issue facing liberal democracies today "concerns the integration of immigrant minorities as citizens of pluralistic democracies" (Fukuyama, 2006, p. 6), particularly those from traditionally illiberal societies. This problem seems more stacked-up for many European countries. "Even with no new net immigration—which most European countries by now have cut off—higher birth rates among minority immigrant communities will increase their overall proportion in the population in the next generation" (Fukuyama, 2006, p. 6).

The summer of 2015 will go down in history as the season that changed the face of Europe in fundamental ways. The imaginary line that divides East and West has been rendered moribund for good. Even if the change is not so obvious at the moment, it will and in ways that will redefine the traditional conceptions of state sovereignty, national borders and citizenship. The months of June to September of 2015 saw thousands of illegal migrants and refugees from the Middle East, Asia, and North and sub-Saharan Africa surging their way, having crossed over through Greece or the Mediterranean Sea, to reach the European heartland. "Not since the second world war has the continent faced refugee or migrant flows of such complexity and scale; aided by smugglers exploiting political conflicts in Libya, Syria, Iraq and others" (*The Economist*, 2015, p. 41). Most are presented as asylum seekers, economic migrants and sojourners of all types of persuasions fleeing from conflicts in Libya, Iraq, Yemen, Somali, Afghanistan and Syria. But thousands from many relatively safe places such as Myanmar, Sudan, Eritrea, Bangladesh, Pakistan, Ivory Coast, Guinea, Mali, Senegal, Nigeria and many others have joined the fray in the inexorable march to the hitherto elusive European conquest. The United Nations High Commissioner for Refugees indicates that of the 320,000 migrants who have reached Europe this year, about 49% are from war-torn Syria, 3% from Iraq, 12% are from Afghanistan, and 8% from Eritrea.

The Emerging Cultural Ferment: Requiem Europe?

But despite the numbers, a deeper reflection would suggest that a silent revolution is slowly brewing on the European continent. Many of these migrants are from countries where Christians continue to be persecuted and/or killed, churches are burnt, the Bible is proscribed and Christian missionaries are harassed and jailed and also prevented from preaching the gospel. Many of the countries are non-secular and do not believe or practice the separation of church and state; the Koran is their dictum, and the sharia is their law; their cultural values about women, crime and punishment are totally different and are very much at odds with that of predominantly Judeo-Christian Europe. There is also the certainty or the greater likelihood that most Middle-Eastern Muslim countries would not have allowed similarly situated Christian refugees or migrants into their own countries under similar or contrary circumstances, but Europe has opened its doors to what inevitably may work to its own detriment as a culture and as a people.

Evidently, the resiliency and portent of the cultural divide can be seen among the traveling migrants themselves even before they reach Europe, such as when "Muslims who were among those trying to get to Italy in a boat in April 2015 threw fellow passengers overboard—drowning 12 of them in the Mediterranean Sea—simply because they were Christians" (Messia et al., 2015, p. 1). The 12 victims were from Nigeria and Ghana, but their killers were Muslims from the Ivory Coast, Mali and Senegal; ironically, they were all heading to and seeking refuge in predominantly Christian countries of Europe. Furthermore, countries such as Libya, Afghanistan, Syria, Sudan, Saudi Arabia and Iraq are a few of the countries where terrorist groups have originated or trained to perpetrate attacks in the West or against Western interests in other parts of the world. It is just as possible that terrorist groups have already infiltrated the ranks of the refugees and will use that as a guise to reach and embed themselves and their infrastructure into the belly of Europe.

While the time of reckoning may be somewhat remote now, what should be less in doubt is that European countries may have wittingly or unwittingly planted the seeds that will eventually lead to dramatic economic, socio-cultural, and political consequences. Opponents of the sudden immigrant surge argue that what the jihad could not do under the gaze of the sword it would now do through waves of willful refugees using women and children to generate sympathy while crashing through the borders of Europe with brazen impunity. They see this as an ideological mission using seemingly hapless migrants aided by naive Western liberal idealism to foster a theocratic project for which the ultimate end is a global Islamic conquest. Scenes of Syrian migrants fighting and refusing police orders at a suburban train station outside Budapest do not allay these concerns, including demonstrations and protests at Budapest's Keleti train station, migrants walking along rail lines in protest while demanding to proceed to Germany and Sweden without going through the normal entry processing required by EU immigration and asylum-seeking laws; and impeding passenger train traffic through the English Channel at the French port of Calais as migrants attempt to cross through the Chunnel in a desperate dash for the United Kingdom.

The Washington Post of September 12, 2015 (online) reports a terse statement and warning credited to the Hungarian Prime Minister, Viktor Orbán, on the future that may now be staring Europe in the face in the behavior of the migrants: "They seized railway stations, rejected giving fingerprints, failed to cooperate and are unwilling to go to places where they would get food, water, accommodation and medical care. They rebelled against Hungarian legal order." Many warn that these events should serve as a foreboding to their likely European hosts of what the future may hold for country and society. For many, the cultural conquest of Europe was won even before it began, ironically abetted willfully by its own political leaders and the people in pursuit of a romanticized idealism of a humane world of mutual coexistence between and across different cultural divides.

By the time the trend runs its course, new cultural and political dynamics would have reshaped for good the socio-cultural and geopolitical character of the European landscape as well as its citizenship. Its ultimate prize would be the annulment of the oft-discussed European identity and ownership of the land. The existing political borders would have been reduced to practical insignificance—they would only exist on the map of Atlas books for weary students in elementary school classrooms. It would not only be Germany but all of Europe where "new arrivals would simply up the ante as soon as they are relocated, exploiting the passport-free Schengen area to rejoin families in Sweden, find work in Germany" (*The Economist*, 2015, p. 42) or move on to other parts of Europe. Even if Germany, Sweden and France were the only countries to take the migrants and refugees, it would not be the end of a beginning; rather it could only be the beginning of a beginning.

In addition, the allure of European social welfarism has added to the attraction. For instance, "in Germany, registered migrants are lodged and fed, their children are cared for and attend school, adults are entitled to about €143 euros a month of pocket money, an additional €216 euros to cover basic needs, and medical costs are free" (Bender and Boston, 2015, p. A6). Ironically, while Hungary, Poland, Czech, the Baltic States and a few others may be reluctant to take in these migrants, once they get into any of the Schengen countries, they will eventually have the unrestrained opportunity to migrate and live in Poland, Hungary, the Czech Republic and the others if they so choose. The migrants are not seeking to move to and live in Germany, Sweden or France; they are, in fact, moving to live in Europe writ large.

While most still live in the yesterday "world of Immanuel Kant, in which 'perpetual peace' was guaranteed by a set of cultural conventions, consensually agreed rules and a belief in the virtues of social solidarity overseen by a redistributive state" (Stephens, 2015, p. A11), such a belief never took into consideration the difficulty of reconciling resilient religious and cultural traditions. The Kantian peace argument was driven more by a concern for continental European peace in a cultural world founded on similarities both in tradition and on Judeo-Christendom. This argument falls apart when used as a placeholder to bridge inter- and intra-cultural differences between societies far removed from the European ethnographic frame of reference. Today, "Neo-Nazi groups in Germany have torched asylum-seekers' hostels; an anti-immigrant group is now the most popular political party in Sweden; as many eastern European countries fear that outsiders will bring in unwelcome values and habits, and Hungary warns that illegal immigrants threaten the nation's survival" (Messia, Borghese and Hanna, 2015). "As Hungary builds a fence across its border with Serbia to keep out illegal immigrants, *ban-the-burqa* debates have sprung up across the Baltic States which together will accept about 725 refugees" (Messia, Borghese and Hanna, 2015).

Nonetheless, the surge in asylum-seekers seems to have tested Europe's commitment to its welcoming ideals. What is most certain is that to the extent that it portends enduring economic and socio-political challenges, the debate about European citizenship and entitlement will continue for the foreseeable future. Is citizenship an entitlement by birth, a moral obligation, a universal natural right or sovereign right, or has it become anything for anybody at a time and place of their own choosing? Because most Western liberal democracies have chosen to gloss over the ensuing tension with benign indifference to the true meaning of citizenship both in substance and in its geopolitical appeal, new and potential immigrants have therefore chosen to define it for them. The sovereign borders and national laws sanctioning entry and exit will no longer be of consequence as they can now be tactically breached with reckless abandon.

In all of these developments there will be consequences, but the full scope of the ramifications may have to wait much longer. If and when the dust settles, what would be certain is that either a constructive outcome results from this both for Europe and the rest of the world, or a worse outcome leads to increased tension over issues of cultural and religious differences and the role of the liberal state in the lives and religious persuasions of European citizens. Whichever way this phenomenon shakes out, what will become most evident in the years ahead is that the first major step to a continental cultural revolution akin to what Karl Polanyi calls *The Great Transformation* will have already taken place. It will either be the beginning of a de facto "global citizenship," the end of national borders, global residency rights for all and increasing ambiguity about the nature of the state or the end of citizenship as we have come to know and understand it. As an inescapable fact of contemporary history, the ramifications for Europe will be most compelling and profound.

Meanwhile, the Arab and Muslim countries, particularly of the Middle East, are more than happy to lay back and let Europe sort out what, in fact, beyond the humanitarian aspect of it, is more of a regional problem of the Middle East than that of Europe. They have feigned silence but strategic indifference as long as Europe continues to take in the burdens of the Middle East, a burden that obviously would never be reciprocated. Many of the wealthy Middle Eastern countries have shied away from taking in the migrants and refugees. Saudi Arabia was said to have taken approximately only 100 to 200 refugees out of millions spread all over the region seeking rescue. Kuwait was said to have taken none. These and the other Muslim countries are aware that a sizeable influx of Muslims into all parts of Europe would in the coming decades, or even by the turn of the century give them a powerful cultural and geopolitical stake in the Europe of the future for all time. The logic that drives their seeming indifference to the plight of the refugees and migrants is premised on a strategic rather than humanitarian foundation.

The German Chancellor Angela Merkel's 'open-door' policy, though enviably idealistic and compassionate, may have shown a serious misunderstanding of the logic and the potential power calculus that drives the migrant and refugee surge. In fact, instead of resolving or stabilizing the problem, evidence has continued to show that the policy has only succeeded in exacerbating it. The unquestionable reality is that Europe's 'humanitarian' gesture will not pacify Muslim or Middle Eastern angst and reservations against Europe and Western civilization, at least, in light of its foreign policy in the region—a foreign policy for which the center of gravity has always been the Israeli and the Palestinian question. In the end, the long but inevitable transformation of Europe can only usher in two competing possibilities—a peaceful coexistence induced by a convergence of values, or a fateful separation anchored on divergence of aspirations, the former more benign; the latter more painful and disastrous.

It should also be noted that what drove the recent tidal wave of migrants and refugees from the Middle East and elsewhere was the coming together of two political trajectories that eventually metamorphosed over the course of several years. The more remote but original cause was the US-Iraq war of 2003 that led to the overthrow of Saddam Hussein and the ruling Baath Party in Iraq. Since then, Iraq has remained an ungovernable powder keg with the rise of the Islamic State (ISIS) as a wild card. The second more proximate causal event was the Arab Spring, which started in Tunisia in 2010 and quickly spread to the rest of North Africa and other countries in the Middle East. By the time it was over, the flamboyant Libyan strongman Muammar Gaddafi was dead, Iraq remained restive and deadly and Syria was turned into a fiery cauldron. All three events created the critical vacuum and political disequilibrium that essentially partitioned the various territories into warring clans of restless heroes and villains. Turkey, Jordan and surrounding countries became the recipients of thousands of 'temporary visitors' that they could not handle alone. From the precipitous invasion of Iraq in 2003 to the protest movements and political upheavals that mutated into the Arab Spring, a refugee and migrant crisis was born, and for better or worse, Europe must now bear the full brunt for years to come.

Competing Issues of Immigration and Identity in the Liberal State

While the increasing migration, movement of labor and capital across international borders may have created economic advantages for some countries, the world will sooner or later have to deal with such fundamental issues as identity and the emergence of hybrid communities in host countries. For example, it has been agued by some economists that the current influx of migrants and refugees into Germany would help provide the labor force and skill needed to grow the economy, especially in recognition of the fact that about one-third of the German population will be older than 65 years by 2060; hence, Germany will need to have more people working in order to be able to pay pensions and care for its elderly (Adams, 2015, p. A6). But "while that sounds promising for Germany's economy, it tells only part of the story. Many of the young able Syrian refugees want to bring families left behind; and they could include elderly parents or young children requiring expensive social services" (Adams, 2015, p. A6). Hence, the expected economic incentive and benefit would have been taken back by the same migrant population that helped to generate it. For a phenomenon that may have far-reaching consequences for decades in the future, it may be very difficult to put a real and accurate price tag on all of this, and there may be social and political costs for which no monetary value will suffice.

Multiculturalism: Adapting a New Ethos

Ironically, while liberal societies seek the integration and assimilation of immigrant cultures into the larger national framework of citizenship, its parallel pursuit and emphasis on multiculturalism reinforces specific cultural identities that take away from the very focus on national integration. Multiculturalism recognizes differences in the make-up of the national community while integration seeks to subsume such differences in the quest for a universal identity. When new immigrants seek to retain their cultural identifications and to move into areas more popularly inhabited by some of 'their own,' they form "hybrid communities" which in itself, reinforce the existing problem of adaptation and assimilation. How to begin to address these is the governance challenge facing contemporary states in a seemingly globalizing international system.

Human migration between countries has been with us over the course of thousands of years. For the past few decades, there has been an increasing level of immigration from Asia and the Middle East to Western and Eastern Europe and from Central and South America to the United States and Canada. Because modern immigrants seek to define and maintain their cultural identities in their host countries, they seek *adaptation* rather than *assimilation.* As new immigrants refuse to completely abandon their heritage to the attraction of Western civilization, their insistence on remaining true to their faith and traditions will emerge as the new source of intrastate conflict, which by extension could provide an 'ideological' basis for the kind of self-justification and radical fundamentalism needed to undermine the cultural and national security interests of host countries.

Many of the conventional reasons cited for why people decide to leave their states of origin range from economic, political, religious and cultural. What distinguishes this era of increasing desire to emigrate is that the international environment (mostly among liberal democracies) has changed and no longer fully views immigration as a matter of right, but partly a humanitarian issue. The immigration of earlier era was mostly legal and officially documented, but a sizeable proportion of today's immigration is illegal. While earlier immigrants arrived with a genuine sense of purpose and a renewed dedication to their new country, the potential for illegal immigration to offer a conduit for terrorist elements to move across international borders with the intent to harm has increased over the years. Many illustrative cases of the unfolding situation abound.

The ethnic makeup of the United States is changing very rapidly, as all the recent migrants have come from Asia, Mexico, the Middle East, Central America and the Caribbean, as a result of the lowering of immigration barriers since the 1960s and especially since the mid-1980s. While many have argued that immigrant identification with their native homelands would have serious consequences for America's national cohesion and civic culture, such critics of the rising tide of ethnic identification are often rearticulating an old American fear that the devotion to ancestral homelands further exacerbates domestic ethnic strains and endangers the fabric of American society. Rising unemployment in many industrial countries has also led to resentment against immigrant populations who flock to these countries for employment and other economic and welfare opportunities. To the extent that the word 'globalization' could offer a normative argument for unrestrained immigration, it may, in fact, lead to more conflicts among and within societies. But of equal importance is the issue of identity and how the state can be more receptive to 'alien' cultures in the search for a reasonable pathway to national integration.

Unfortunately, rather than fostering practical propositions on the issue of identity, the contemporary debate has been reduced to a level of ideological romanticism bereft of effective solutions for dealing with the problem of cultural assimilation and citizenship. As Francis Fukuyama (2006, p. 18) argues, "the problem of immigration and identity ultimately converges with the larger problem of the valuelessness of postmodernity, which in itself, has made it impossible for them to assert the kinds of shared beliefs for which they demand as a condition for citizenship." "Multiculturalism, understood not just as tolerance of cultural diversity in de facto multicultural societies but as the demand for legal recognition of the rights of ethnic, racial, religious, or cultural groups, has now become established in virtually all modern liberal democracies" (Fukuyama, 2006, p. 9). Not only does multiculturalism require a noticeable re-arrangement in the traditional institutions of socio-political relations, it also requires an equivalent reorientation and change in the essential foundations of national identity.

The question remains as to whether multiculturalism can create the kind of 'high citizenship' in the interest of the *polis* that was required in the Aristotelian tradition or whether it simply shifts hitherto existent political and economic competition into the cultural arena. Multiculturalism recognizes differences in the political character of citizenship while at the same time seeking to interpret such differences in the context of national identity. "By celebrating 'difference,' identity politics raises questions about what defines us as a nation" (Citrin et al., 2007, p. 31). For most new immigrants, it is a rather painful experience to abandon the culture and customs they have grown up in; while for the native citizens, continued emphasis on multiculturalism and its reference to 'diversity' raises more questions about identity. What does this mean for my own native culture? What does it means for my identity, and do I have to learn the culture of the 'other' in order to retain portions of mine? As hybrid communities develop in host countries, they may, in fact, force societies to reevaluate contemporary ideas of citizenship as well as the very concept of statehood. These are both vexing questions that in many practical ways have remained the bane of multiculturalism.

The Political Economy of Labor and Capital Movements

It has been said that labor migration from poorer to richer countries oftentimes creates a reverse-transfer of capital as workers send periodic remittances back to their home countries. This has helped, in fundamental ways, to sustain a sizeable proportion of the domestic economy. In addition, although "some of the migration may reflect traditional migratory patterns among tribes cutting across modern postcolonial nation-states" (Bhagwati, 1988, p. 155), it is the evolving cultural attachment and residential patterns that make this a lasting phenomenon. As skilled and unskilled workers from less developed and, in most cases, culturally distinct 'nation-states' transplant themselves from less-developed to developed economies, they evolve into a unique economic category and hence may reflect a mutual-gain transaction between governments of the sending and receiving countries. For its seemingly small size, however, this development raises a few concerns relating to the loss of skilled nationals to foreign, often richer nations—converting the phenomenon of skilled migration into the problem of the 'brain drain' (Bhagwati, 1988, p. 163).

By sending remittances to families and relatives in their native countries, immigrants (skilled and unskilled) also engage in the process of capital transfers or global financial flows. "These capital flows augment domestic savings and can contribute to investment, growth, financial sector development, technology transfer and poverty reduction" (Goldin and Reinert, 2006, p. 70). However, there is evidence that capital flows may entail potential costs that are larger than in the case of normal trade transactions and tend to create economic dislocations or adjustments in the host countries that may negatively impact on the poor and unemployed. Increasing unemployment and joblessness in the host country is more often than not blamed on the new immigrants' taking jobs that host citizens could have taken. The social resentment and the attendant backlash generally result in increased calls for immigration regulation, distrust of aliens, neglect and marginalization in policy making and program implementation.

As immigrant communities evolve into new class systems, they seek to augment their newfound economic relevance with increased agitation for political participation, representation and inclusive citizenship. "In the modern age, however, states have grown more resistant to conferring citizenship upon foreigners who lack a connection to the national cultural identity" (Goldin and Reinert, 2006, p. 158). Today's migrants, for one reason or another, do so with the ultimate intent to resettle in their host countries. Accentuating this phenomenon is the "immigration regimes of the richer countries that seek out economic migrants who possess desirable socioeconomic characteristics. "For Australia, Canada, and New Zealand, this is achieved through the points system—which grants permanent residence to applicants who offer the right mix of skills, capital and adaptability. The United States, on the other hand, assigns annual quotas to categories of 'persons of extraordinary ability' eligible for permanent residence" (Goldin and Reinert, 2006, p. 158). Suffice it then to say that many of these people eventually become citizens of their host countries, but they do so more for the economic and political conveniences they offer, while still living truthfully to the cultural foundations of their native countries. As immigration and shifting residential patterns continue to dilute the distinction between citizens and aliens, how can contemporary states adjust or, at best, manage the complex issues of cultural pluralism and the attendant demand for group equality?

The Emerging Fault Line: Power Politics and Territorial Conquest

The idea of a transnationalist threat to American unity has also received renewed interest from the writings of Samuel Huntington concerning the persistence of "kin-country" syndrome and "diaspora" loyalties among new immigrant populations. "In the post-Cold War era, diasporic communities which are intensely involved in the prolonged conflicts of their kin countries and/or communities muster considerable political influence over their host governments, redefine their national interest, and affect perceptions of identity in both their old and new countries of residence" (Huntington, 1996, pp. 272–291). "Massive immigration (legal and illegal) from Mexico and the new trend toward rapprochement and reconciliation between the Mexican government and Mexican-Americans have also raised some anxiety over Mexican political separatism in America" (Tololyan, 1991, p. 36). Mexican-Americans make up the majority of the US Hispanic community, which has now become the largest ethnic minority in the country. "In Houston, the nation's fourth largest city, Hispanics have overtaken 'Anglo-Americans' as the city's largest ethnic group, largely because of immigration from Mexico" (*Washington Post*, 1998). To the extent that this level of immigration benefits Mexico by allowing it to export its own domestic problems (including unemployment) elsewhere, transnationalism has important political implications for both countries. Not only does it contribute to domestic electoral opportunities in the United States when candidates appeal to new demographic trends within their constituency, it also serves as source of indirect influence on US foreign policy and international relations.

Given that by 2050 white America is expected to lose its majority to Hispanics, Asians and blacks, Huntington wonders whether the trend toward 'the de-Westernization of the United States means its de-Americanization in the democratic sense.' He warns that, if the pillars of American identity—the democratic liberal principle and its European heritage—are further eroded, the United States might find itself, like the former Soviet Union, falling "onto the ash heap of history." With an ever-increasing birthrate including legal and illegal immigration, the new immigrant population is poised to shape not only the demographic characteristics of the United States, but also its national identity and politics. The enormous constitutional protections offered by liberal free societies provide a legal basis for new immigrants to challenge and in most cases reverse the existing state of affairs in their host countries.

A case in point would be the State of Texas, in which it has been noted that Hispanics make up more than a majority of students in the public school system. In June 2005 and to much public dismay, the Dallas (TX) public school system made a proposal that all principals of its public schools must learn to speak Spanish (perhaps as a first language), so as to be able to communicate more effectively with a majority of its students and their parents. The proposal stands as one of many incremental but seemingly mundane changes that will visit many parts of the United States as well as Europe—as immigrant populations acquire demographic and political majorities at different governmental levels.

While it remains difficult to accurately estimate the number of illegal immigrants in the United States, most data locate it at 11 million, the greater majority of which are Mexicans. Compared to the general American population, "illegal immigrants are less educated, more likely to work in agriculture, construction, and other low-wage jobs, more likely to speak Spanish, and more likely to live in ethnic enclaves. Hence, they are less likely than other immigrants or native-born Hispanics to become integrated into mainstream society or to view themselves as members of the American political community" (Citrin et al., 2007, p. 46). Statistics show that "about 6.3 million illegal immigrants from Mexico live in the United States, and an average of 485,000 more arrive each year. In response, state legislatures considered nearly 300 bills on immigration policy in the first half of 2005 alone, but passed only 47" (Thornburgh, 2006, p. 38), thus pointing to the political nature and difficulty of making immigration policy even at a time when homeland security has remained the centerpiece of national security strategy.

Evidence points to the fact that most of the illegal immigrants who come into the United States have settled in the border states of Texas, Arizona and California and in others such as New Mexico, Florida and Colorado. In a few years, a combination of legal and illegal immigration and high birth rates among these populations will grant them enough votes to elect representatives from their own communities into positions of political power. And the figures are indeed rather impressive. Not only do 11 million people live in the United States illegally; the 41 million Hispanics living in the country, legally or not, are the nation's largest minority. "Former Caucasian majorities in Miami and Los Angeles have become minorities; and in another ten years, the same will likely be true of New York and Washington, DC" (Mascolo, 2006, p. 3). Over time, they would be able to acquire enough numbers to become the majority and to reshape the political, economic and cultural landscape in these states and communities. The cultural attachment (kin-country syndrome) will continue to strengthen the bond of fellowship between immigrants and their native countries.

The fault lines are already evident in many other ways, such as the move by some states to require English as the official language (a reaction to bilingual education), the singing of the national anthem in Spanish without the words as they are in the original version, printing public documents or signposts in many other languages besides English; and mandating employees to learn to speak the language of their benefactors and other incremental changes. As this phenomenon plays itself out over the next few decades, it will become a deciding factor in the evolving battle of identity, cultural dominance, territorial and political control. The irony is that even if illegal immigration is completely brought to a halt today, the dynamic enunciated above has already become inevitable and would simply be reinforced by a high birth rate and changing residential patterns.

Once Upon a Time: Sunset for the American Empire?

In his much acclaimed book titled *Sorrows of Empire*, Chalmers Johnson (2004) decried the impending demise of American global hegemony by recollecting a trail of foreign policy and grand strategic blunders the United States has made over the years and how the cumulative effect has already set the stage for America's decline. It was an apocalyptic assessment of an impending disintegration of the American empire such that even "if the likelihood of perpetual war hangs over the world, the situation in the United States hardly seems any better" (Johnson, 2004, p. 291). By referencing the demise of six earlier empires: those of Nazi Germany, Imperial Japan, Great Britain, France, the Netherlands and the Soviet Union, Johnson (2004, p. 310) denotes that while "empires do not last, their ends are usually unpleasant" and that the reason for their collapse can be tied to a combination of imperial overstretch, rigid economic institutions and an inability to reform, which left them vulnerable in the face of disastrous wars. Johnson (2004, p. 310) therefore concludes that "there is no reason to think that an American empire will not go the same way—and for the same reasons."

Nonetheless, one should not be particularly bothered by the historical relativism inherent in Johnson's predictions. Instead, I argue that the impending 'demise' of the American state is less likely to be the result of its "militarism and imperialism which threatens democratic government at home just as they menace the independence and sovereignty of other countries" (Johnson, 2004, p. 291). If the mighty Soviet Union could collapse so inexorably in 1991 without a single shot being fired by either of the Cold War adversaries, the predicted collapse of the American empire should not seem so earth-shattering. After all there was a Roman Empire, and years after that the British Empire. That was a time when kings and monarchs ruled many regions of the world by a combination of imperial majesty and brute subjugation. What will eventually undermine and (even if slowly) set the stage for an eventual 'demise' of the American empire, its national identity and, in fact, its sovereignty, would be unchecked illegal immigration. Its long-term implications for the extant social and political structure, national interest and domestic policy will be highly consequential.

As the political interests of immigrant communities slowly diverge from those of the national government (or the dominant political culture), the momentum to seek a kind of political separation (political identity or self-determination) from the national government will start to build up. They can then be able to use their electoral votes to affect the kinds of structural and political changes they seek. Even if this does not prove possible, there is that other greater (and perhaps more proximate) possibility that border states like Texas, California, Arizona and even New Mexico, will eventually become part of a "Greater Mexico," perhaps within the next 20 to 40 years. If and when a democratic and free-market regime emerges in Cuba in the next couple of years, there is a fair amount of certainty that Florida will become part of a 'Greater Cuba.' If this socio-political engineering is repeated in many other states and regions in the United States, it begins a process in which the body politic starts to disintegrate, and the American national character and identity as we know it becomes irrecoverable.

Because "identities are not only formed by groups seeking recognition, but also by groups that seek domination" (Isin and Wood, 1999, p. 15), it underscores a level of emotional intensity that groups bring to bear on matters of cultural interest and superiority. The real question remains as to how we govern under this new system and arrangement, and how traditional identities and the existing social structure can be made to conform to the unfolding changes. While illegal immigration remains a judicial, security and economic problem for the United States, unfortunately, the premise from which policy makers see it is through the narrative of electoral and partisan politics. This is why the state, with all its might, has been unable to reclaim the sovereign authority over its borders.

Hybrid Communities: Cultural Enclaves in Search of Identity

As can be observed in the United States, many immigrant populations have been quite successful in carving out for themselves their own territory from the larger American real estate pie. Once in the country, they 'naturally' gravitate to areas where there already exist specific cultural enclaves similar to theirs and settle down for good. They surround themselves with traditional and cultural artifacts from their home countries as a symbol of identity as well as affinity. For much the same reason migrants are attracted to countries where other migrants from their home communities have settled, migrants also tend to cluster in particular industries and occupations (Goldin and Reinert, 2006). In some cases, industries become dependent on migrant labor to survive and remain competitive.

For instance in the early 1960s, the US Department of Labor found that around 85% of the 670,000 farmworkers in the United States were immigrants, many of whom were undocumented (Gabbard et al., 1994). Western European farmers have recruited Eastern Europeans who enter on tourist visas but work as agricultural laborers, and many developed countries have come to depend on migrant labor to help meet shortfalls in various sectors, including medicine, information technology, education, health, engineering and a host of other occupational categories (Stalker, 2001). The Chinatowns, the barrios and various ethnic enclaves in many urban centers are good examples of resilient subcultures within the larger American cultural domain. Many have also argued that "even when those newcomers become citizens, group-oriented policies like the amended Voting Rights Act and bilingual education encourage them to identify as members of racial and ethnic groups rather than as members of the entire American people" (Shain, 1999, p. 5).

As their populations increase, they will over time acquire enough voting power to reshape the political fate of their host countries in fundamental ways that can only provoke greater resistance and a sense of cultural ambiguity and loss in the host populations. The current cultural tension in France as it struggles to maintain its secularity in the face of Muslim advocacy for religious preferences has sent shock waves to other countries in Western Europe of the impending crisis they will face with an increasing Muslim population. In addition to being perceived as a threat to the cultural coherence of the host country, transnational immigration is also viewed as a challenge to state sovereignty and its security.

Figure 8.1 offers a portrait that illuminates the dynamic at work in most countries as forces of differentiation and consolidation work in tandem to bridge potential conflicts between immigrant and native populations. As immigrant populations move into specific regions or communities in their host countries, the need for territorial expansion arises as more and more cluster in the same area. The socioeconomic and cultural changes puts more pressure on the existing social and economic relations by moving beyond the *zone of toleration and accommodation*—beyond which native or host populations begin to notice dramatic changes and shifts in the existing status quo. In many countries and states like the Southwest of the United States, Berlin (Germany), Great Britain, Spain and Italy, this development is generally accompanied by a degree of political ascendancy and relevance of the 'alien' population. In response, community and interest groups and ordinary citizens of host countries put up a *zone of resistance* (brick walls) through either legislative advocacy or immigration regulation as a way of checkmating the impending cultural shift in their lifestyle and identity. The space between the *zone of toleration* and *zone of resistance* offers opportunity for negotiation and accommodation, but if and when the boundary is breached beyond the 'zone of resistance,' the resultant conflict ordinarily manifests itself into resentment and/or overt violence against 'alien' communities.

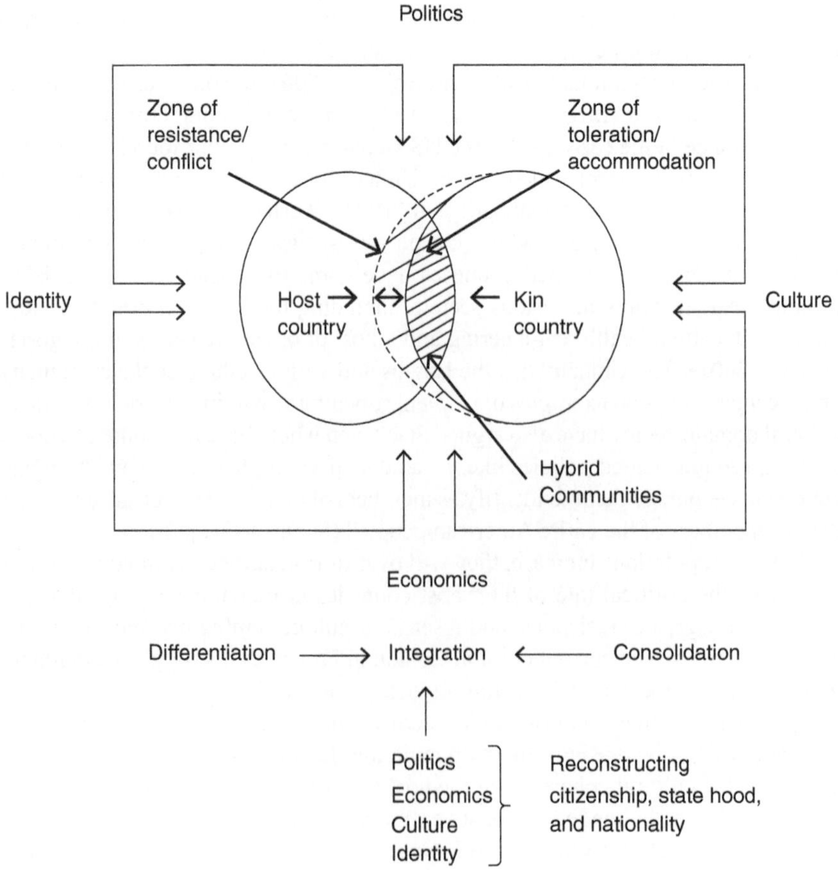

Figure 8.1 Competing Norms of Cultural Consolidation and Differentiation.

The issues at stake become more manifest and pronounced as both sides draw more deeply upon the reality and prospects of the unfolding situation and what it may mean for their traditional conception of citizenship, nationality and statehood. The ideal of national integration, therefore, reflects a patchwork of agreements based on celebrating cultural differences, on the one hand, and consolidating commonalities on the other. It is therefore the degree of divergence between these 'differences and commonalties' that determines the extent to which national integration takes or does not take place.

Globalization is about change, but it is a unique form of change that differentiates in the same way that it consolidates. While it may succeed in "bringing various cultural communities together, creating large areas of overlap and convergence; it also creates conditions which, in most cases, also threatens the cultural identity of societies—causing a sense of panic that militates against common dialogue" (Parekh, 2008, p. 181). As the state endures despite globalization, "one indication of belongingness is citizenship which, in and of itself, harbors a persistent appeal that lies in the energy and passion that those who possess it devote to in keeping it to themselves and excluding others from it" (Croucher, 2004, p. 62). As citizenship claims morph into the struggle for identity, the inchoate politics of accommodation slowly transcends a politics of exclusion. In many host communities, citizens and interest groups have gotten into what might be described as a "push-back" mode, as a way of stopping further erosion and modification of their national character, identity and way of life. The choice for states is to devise new methods for managing immigration and sovereignty in such a way that inherent tensions are not manifested in overt backlash and cultural conflict between native and foreigner. The extent to which this is successful will depend on how new structures of governance and reconceptualization of identity and citizenship are accepted in the evolving cultural pluralism of contemporary states.

9 Citizenship Beyond Borders

Quo Vadis?

It would seem that the world of the twenty-first century is a world of change and flux, but like centuries long gone, the contemporary world is also a restless one. The increasing application of information technology and digital communications has opened up new possibilities for the exchange of information and transportation, and provides greater comfort and ease in the way traditional functions are carried out. As people and cultures of the world come together in terms of increased transborder transportation, immigration and changing residential patterns, the traditional idea of national borders becomes increasingly challenged. The state as we know it has always been the basis for inclusion and exclusion by virtue of the presence of national borders that demarcate one state from the other, but as these seemingly become more irrelevant in our new condition, the ideal of the state itself must of necessity come under intense pressure. It is in this regard that the issue of global citizenship has become the new idealism in contemporary discourse on the subject matter of citizenship. Global citizenship has become a growing fad, "much more than an abstract or seemingly elusive ideal, espoused mainly by assumed intellectuals and visionaries" (Schattle, 2008, p. 159)—to the effect that the ideal is a form of self-awareness and a shared consciousness or state of mind among persons either in their own self-reflection of the world around them or in their engagement with others in the mainstream of public discourse.

Global Citizenship: A Bridge Too Far

Part of the argument rests on the weak premise that increased communication and transportation have facilitated transcultural immigration, and the Internet has also opened up much greater information about understanding the world from Lusaka in Zambia to Anchorage in Alaska, and many more in between. As a result, people and cultures are getting closer to each other and sharing different types of information and aspirations that were not available a few years ago. The irony is that "people are not coming together in the political or cultural sense of the term; and the Internet, although it may have increased the frequency and speed of cross-cultural communication, has not necessarily brought about the homogenization of cultures" (Kalu, 2007, p. 298)—a critical ingredient for the realization of the norms that would undergird global citizenship. In most cases, the Internet has become an unwilling vehicle for the disintegration of cultures, relentlessly infusing them with alien traditions, new inventions and puerile vices that were never a recognized aspect of the extant social values and practices.

Furthermore, the ideal of global citizenship presupposes a relatively 'peaceful' world, a world in which there is an increasing momentum toward shared values and aspirations, in which common sense and respect for a more durable future is the general norm. It is also an idea that suggests a climate of 'open borders,' one in which a 'world state' could possibly replace existing independent states as the institutional anchor for the types of rights and entitlements consistent with global citizenship. In a realist world where anarchy reigns supreme, and where "rules governing international behavior are generally flaunted by member states when matters of state sovereignty and national interest collide with the collective will of the international community" (Kalu, 2007, p. 303); how we govern the global estate, by whom and under what conditions remain the unanswered questions. Under the current system each state maintains its sovereignty and citizenship, yet there is so much conflict and acrimony between and within states. How much worse would it be when states come together under the ideal of global citizenship, even if as a normative construct? Would that be more benign than what we have today?

While I agree that there may, in fact, be some virtue in the ideal of global citizenship, it still begs the question as to its practicality. While "global citizenship and cosmopolitanism are seen in part as sets of moral understandings that give emphasis to attributes common to all individuals, regardless of their national or other group affiliations" (Cabrera, 2010, p. 13), the problem becomes more manifest in a world where ethno-cultural categories remain more obdurate and resilient than any type of grand idealistic future that can be mustered. There is also the moral corollary to global citizenship in the sense that "all individuals are said to be equal at some fundamental level, and their equality is to be recognized or respected because of their status as human beings, rather than according to any status ascribed to them as members of an identity set" (Cabrera, 2010, p. 14; Held, 2005). As noteworthy as this argument is, it still falls flat when considered in light of the fact that the concept of equality has many variants—such as economic, political, judicial, social and cultural equalities—each of which draws upon different national histories, experiences, economic relationships and types of political associations or regimes. Hence, to what extent is the concept and understanding of *equality* in the United States the same as in North Korea, China, Russia, Malaysia, Bhutan or Guatemala?

The International System and Structural Inequalities

The international system is made up of states of relative equality and states of relative inequality. The "basic structure of the international system largely determines how states think and act toward each other" (Mearsheimer, 2001, p. 369). Because inequality abounds in many areas of the international system, one is unsure as to how the ideal of global citizenship would appeal to all states as a universal norm and practice. While the international market regime reinforced by the ethos of liberal institutionalism has tended to encourage economic interdependence among states as a means of preserving a more stable mutually beneficial and peaceful international order, the reality is that there remains an ever-growing gulf between rich and poor nations. This can be seen in such global indicators as the Human Development Index, literacy, indebtedness, e-government index, GDP per capita, gross national income per capita and the Gini index.

In the same way that "economic interdependence has the tendency to reinforce the asymmetrical trade relations between rich and poor states, it also has not reduced the rise in relative poverty and deprivation among many developing countries" (Kalu, 2007, p. 309). Rather, what has become most obvious is that many of the developing countries do not have the economies of scale or comparative advantage critical to competition in the international market regime. Additionally, the undiversified nature of their primary exports adds to their competitive disadvantage. While it is a fairly well-known fact that the "industrialization prospects of an underdeveloped country are frequently judged, and judged adversely, in terms of cheapness of labor as against capital goods and of the resulting difficulty in substituting scarce capital for abundant labor; the reality is that conditions will vary from industry to industry and from country to country" (Gerschenkron, 1962, pp. 8–9). In this regard, countries develop at different paces and in different historical times and under different technological and material constraints.

In essence, there is among nations less of a shared identity that could be used as a permanent foundation for the kind of global citizenship premised on the general humanity of mankind. The traditional means of establishing citizenship has been as a shared national identity or as an attachment to a particular state. A global citizenship without a specific state would be an identity or property not necessarily based on a universal consensus as to its merit; it would be founded on the ways and means by which states independently interpret and confer specific rights. States generally operate on the basis of self-interest and are unwilling to sacrifice it to other competing interests. To the extent that "we can understand values as based on interests or needs, or given as the goals of specific activities and projects arising from the point of view of particular groups of individuals" (Gould, 2001, p. 79), it is debatable whether "efforts to achieve consensus on generalizable interests or norms will lead to universal agreement" (Gould, 2001, p. 79).

In an anarchic self-help world without a supranational coordinating authority, states rarely trust each other and are apprehensive of what the other states' intentions and inclinations might be. As such, "states always act according to their own self-interest and are reluctant to subordinate their interests to the interest of the international community" (Mearsheimer, 2001, p. 33). It is therefore through the lens of national interest that states would embrace the ideal of global citizenship. Since a state's national interest is generally different from that of other states, it would thus mean that while most states would welcome the ideal for what it is, others would most likely opt for it as long as it advances their national interest. But where this is lacking, the ideal and what it may stand for would be abandoned at the slightest opportunity. "In a world in which the national state is the overwhelming norm, all of this means that states can now be imagined without linguistic communality—not in the naive spirit of *nosotros los Americanos*, but out of a general awareness of what modern history has demonstrated to be possible" (Anderson, 1983, p. 135). As an ideal, global citizenship would thus live a precarious existence.

The State Under Siege

The modern state system is undergoing a relentless siege from both within and without. Even among contemporary thinkers and idealists, there is a constant barrage of new interpretations and reconceptualization regarding what the modern state is, is not, or should be. On the singular premise that no single entity can withstand this much pressure for as long as the state has endured it, at some point in the not so distant future, the pressure will generate its own critical mass. Either the state will succumb to it in one crystalizing burst of energy, or it will fizzle out of its own accord in a slow but gradual process of decline and obsolescence. While everything around it and within it is changing rather rapidly, there has to be a simple realization that the modern state will change from what we know today. For the remainder of this chapter, I will explore the dynamics of that change as well as the factors that will drive it. But what I cannot tell you is whether the world would be better for it or worse. How a common notion of global citizenship will evolve in the midst of the contemporary crisis of intra- and inter-state relations still remains an unknown factor. That is the great uncertainty we will have to live with, for the future presents mankind with an intriguing paradox—one that suggests the promise of great possibilities, and another that stands at the crossroads between endless suspense and purgatory on earth.

From within, criminal gangs have taken over sections of major cities and imposed their law and justice on its inhabitants, laws and regulations are broken at will and law enforcement agencies, so legitimized by the authority of the state to enforce the rule of law in the maintenance of social peace, have unfortunately been made to become the problem rather than the solution. Today, the criminal who willfully breaks the law receives greater public sympathy and has more rights than the law enforcement officer who made the interdiction; hence, as law and order become to each according to your own interpretation, the state continues to unravel at the seams, and everywhere anarchy reigns supreme. The customary norms that have bound the framework of social life and, invariably citizenship, have been sidelined in preference of new seemingly arcane traditions that have no history behind them. The distinction between morality and immorality has become blurred such that the most odious of vices are celebrated as virtue under the hubris of disguised progressivism bereft of a theoretical or moral foundation. As it is currently, state and society both seem to be heading in a direction very few can predict, and they are speeding toward it with reckless abandon.

The political rhetoric of the cliché "big government" has become a household euphemism for an attack on the state as the ruthless and all-encompassing behemoth bent on taking away individual rights as well as imposing more demanding tax regimes on society as a whole. In its lonely and paradoxical situation, the state receives little or no accolade when things are going well and people are happy, but when things go wrong (as they always do), the state and the government in power are visited with an unceasing opprobrium. "Contested issues are adjudicated on the basis of the merits of the case, as defined by international human rights codes, and not on the basis of national interest or how the state defines its scope of jurisdiction" (Jacobson, 1996, p. 119). The news media by virtue of specific constitutional guarantees has essentially taken over the role of setting the state's political agenda by, for better or worse, focusing and reinforcing some issues and not others, but at the same time attacking and impugning the integrity of the state and its institutions at the slightest opportunity. For the state, there is no place to hide.

Criminal cartels within the state in complicity with cartels outside the state have developed a network system of their own that enables them to import drugs, narcotics and adulterated and counterfeit products in contravention of state laws. Within and between states, human trafficking, transborder prostitution, slavery, money laundering, credit card fraud, identity thefts, Internet hacking and all sorts of financial crimes have run amok—and the state does not have the ability to control them. The territorial sovereignty and authority of the state have also come under attack as terrorist groups seize chunks of territory and impose their will on it, including collecting taxes and informal rents from hapless citizens. Children, men, and women under the guidance of terrorist groups can now blow themselves up in a crowd of innocent citizens as long as they take hundreds with them. Instead of celebrating peace profound, the world has become numbed by uncommon violence.

A subterranean economy in the form of currency counterfeiting, child pornography, kidnapping for ransom, sale of previously contraband drugs and other illicit vices have continued to operate in tandem with the formal economy, such that both are now viewed as contributory factors in economic growth and employment. Equally unsparing of itself, the state nonetheless harbors an implicit paradox. While it seeks to serve as an institutional and legal basis for the execution of public polices and the law, it ironically also offers a placeholder for uncommon corruption, hoodlumism and official malfeasance that has seen public funds siphoned away or diverted to serve narrow private interests. High-handed corruption and debauchery has become second nature to the existence of most contemporary states. In a world in which many are more willing than ever to take advantage of the few, how we ever get to celebrate our commonness may stand as the greatest riddle of the century. In our daily encounters, mob rule and elevated agitation have taken over sane discourse in the public space leaving little room for reciprocity and mutual exchange of ideas; and zero-sum game has become the new calculus for engaging competing issues of public policy. The more ominous prospect is that none of these shows any signs of abetting now or in the near future. For better or for worse, most citizens and public officials seem to have accepted it as part of living in the modern state.

In the United States particularly, there are over 200 "sanctuary cities" that harbor and protect people who break the laws of the state and enter the United States illegally and in contravention of federal law. As illustrated by Steve Salvi

(2015), despite a 1996 federal law (the Illegal Immigration Reform and Immigrant Responsibility Act [IIRIRA]) that requires local governments to cooperate with Department of Homeland Security's Immigration and Customs Enforcement (ICE), many large urban cities (and some small) have adopted so-called "sanctuary" policies. Generally, sanctuary policies instruct city employees not to notify the federal government of the presence of illegal aliens living in their communities. The policies also end the distinction between legal resident aliens and illegal aliens—so illegal aliens often benefit from taxpayer-funded government services and programs. The municipal and local authorities purposely undermine the power of the juridical state.

As human traffickers continue to smuggle illegal migrants across state borders with impunity, authorities are also handicapped by their own laws that prevent them from enforcing who comes in and who gets out. State institutions are used to undermine the very policies they are supposed to enforce. And, for this, many citizens have chosen to disengage from the *public* or have remained frustrated at not knowing to what and where they are being herded. Many people will take comfort in not paying their taxes to the state if the possibility of not being caught ever presents itself; and many will free ride on the sacrifices of others where the penalty for not contributing is minimal or non-existent. In the search for absolute freedom and a moralizing idealism that seems to operate above the practical manifestations of the everyday realities of the human condition, one is always reminded of the three words: "What's the catch?" Unfortunately, the modern state and what it stands for is the *catch*. The state is slowly losing its attachment to society and citizenship without knowing it. In a world of unfolding moral decline, where the boundary between decency and vileness is becoming narrower with each passing day, and unfortunately, citizenship cannot be immune nor can it be an exception to the new normal that surrounds it.

After Citizenship: Managing Global Governance

In and of itself, the idea of "global citizenship is problematical, not just in the obvious fact that it has no legal standing yet of any kind, or a governmental body to support and defend it" (Lagos, 2013, p. 162), but the sovereign actions of states in contemporary world politics work at cross-purposes to the very interests global citizenship seeks to represent. Amid a history of recurrent conflicts and rivalry between states, "the Cold War spanned not only military and strategic issues but filtered into competition over the international economy, technology (the race to outer space, nuclear arms race) sports competitions, and virtually all aspects of society" (Quackenbush, 2015, p. 319). Even without any external impulse to the effect, internal disequilibrium within states can also generate their own pathologies. Contemporary examples abound, in the forms of failed state institutions (like Somali, Libya, Yemen), insurgency movements (like the Taliban in Afghanistan and Boko Haram in Nigeria and Cameroon), the economic crisis and market failures like the recent Greek *tragedy* (debt crisis of 2015) and China's stock market crash of 2015 that saw individual and institutional investors lose billions of dollars if not more.

Today, rivalries, competition, outright hostilities and acrimony abound everywhere between and within states: between the United States and Russia over Putin's more muscular foreign policy and militarism regarding Crimea and separatists in Ukraine, between Iran and Saudi Arabia over Yemen and the evolving balance of power in the Middle East, between the United States and Iran over the latter's nuclear brinkmanship, between India and Pakistan over Jammu and Kashmir, between India and China over territories adjoining their common borders, between Israel and the Arab world over the enduring issues of Palestine, between Sunnis and Shias in almost every country where they co-exist, between Sudan and South Sudan, and between North Korea and the rest of the world. Even within countries like Libya, Syria, Iraq, South Sudan, Central African Republic, Yemen, Mali, Burundi and many others, things seem to have fallen apart and the center cannot hold. There was a time when piracy on the high seas was the de facto economic policy of a state (and may still be today), and bruised and battered, the state known as Somali became synonymous with all that can go wrong when state, citizenship and its institutions disconnect from each other.

The restlessness of the global state system remains unabated. Ongoing geostrategic realignments and power balancing has seen a resurgent Russia under Putin as well as a rising China. With one of the world's most powerful growth economies under its control and the continuing flexing of its military muscle in the South Pacific and Asia geostrategic hemisphere, it is unclear whether China's rise will be aggressive or peaceful—adding more uncertainty to the power politics of the post-Cold War era. The current revolution in military affairs (RMAs) and the rise of asymmetric warfare and tactics has made interstate and intrastate conflicts more lethal and deadly with devastating consequences. "When asymmetric warfare is implemented, traditional defensive barriers such as military power and deterrence (that has kept the peace for the last fifty plus years) often declines in value" (Kay, 2015, p. 246). In this regard, the deck of cards is stacked against the state: "Terrorists or insurgents might have no reservation in killing large numbers of innocent civilians; the modern state which often operates under legal, public, and ethical constraints may be enjoined from responding in kind" (Kay, 2015, p. 247).

There is an intriguing paradox that seems to confront humanity on earth. While technological breakthroughs in medicine, nutrition and health care have ended up securing and extending the quality of human life, the same technological breakthroughs have unleashed unto the world so much destructive power, all marshalled for a quick and sudden obliteration of the same humanity that it seeks to preserve. Two atomic bombs were dropped during WW II on Hiroshima and Nagasaki in 1945, and for all the devastation, rather than evoking eternal moments of somber reflection on many countries, the lethality of the bomb has ironically become an endless fatal attraction for many countries as they seek to develop their own nuclear capabilities. They will go to great lengths to get them without thinking much about the potential consequences to their own survival.

As historical animosities and disputes endure and reinvent themselves, they have become the bane of global peace, such that peaceful resolution of conflicts has become a rare commodity. The case can be made that citizenship can exist in a "different axis of social and political life, such as in the relations between individual and the state, in the bonds that link states together in an international society, and in the much looser realm consisting of the ties between individuals and humanity" (Linklater, 2007, p. 76); the last point is very relevant to the argument made earlier as well as the hypothesis I seek to develop in later sections of this chapter. It is even more sobering when we learn that the state of the world in which we wish to embed the moral foundation of global citizenship is a world in which many states are in a seemingly perpetual crisis. While "no one has yet come up with a workable criterion for the identification of a society other than in the context of a state; yet theorists insist on endowing societies with properties such as common culture, values, and a coherent system of social control" (Tilly, 2008, p. 112). Hence "if we are searching for the secret of systematic variation, individualizing and universalizing comparison may help clear the way, but they will not get us very far" (Tilly, 2008, p. 115). The state of world politics is not a safe place, nor does it offer a greater degree of confidence in the sense of a more benevolent context for the exercise of global citizenship, whether construed as a collective consciousness, a norm or as an institution or regime.

The Future World and How It Will Come About

But if there is something for which an agreement is desirable, it is that the modern state as we know it today will change in the future. "If the duality of state and society has been the organizing frame of political debate and practice since, arguably, the Peace of Westphalia in 1648, then there are signs that we are reaching another *Westphalian moment*" (Jacobson, 1998, p. 41). Recent developments have, if nothing else, seemed to undermine existing confidence that the state as currently conceived can endure beyond the next 30 to 50 years, and that is being overly gracious. Today, "we are gradually moving out of a world of sovereign states toward new forms of overlapping jurisdictions" (Carter, 2001, p. 19) as demonstrated in "the growing foreign populations in Western Europe and in the United States, the growing proportion of persons with dual citizenships and multiple state memberships; and the increase in cross-national marriages suggest that traditional models of the melting pot, of a unitary and bounded civil society, are, at best, in question" (Jacobson, 1998, p. 42). Furthermore, the contexts in which the rights of citizenship are claimed and enjoyed and its duties discharged have become more extensive, and the proportion of the population embraced by full civic membership has become vastly expanded as well as differentiated (Heater, 1999, p. 155).

Many people who decide to immigrate to another country oftentimes retain cultural loyalties to their home countries as opposed to their new abodes. For them, and in the "metaphoric as well as in the literal sense, home is somewhere else" (Jacobson, 1998, p. 42). What would this mean for the state as well as global citizenship? As I have already argued, the modern state will change in fundamental ways, and in the same way that everything surrounding and within it has been changing, it would not be an overstatement to suggest that it may, optimistically construed, come to an end within the next 30 or 50 years or even sooner.

On the other hand, the ideal of global citizenship in the substantive sense of the term will be untenable. It is true that there have been individuals and organizations that are often touted as '*global citizens,*' but the premise for that assignment does not exist in substance. I have in mind individuals such as the Secretary-General of the United Nations, Directors of various United Nations agencies like the United Nations Development Program (UNDP), the United Nations Children's Emergency Fund (UNICEF) or Heads of the World Bank and the International Monetary Fund (IMF); non-governmental organizations such as *Médecins Sans Frontières* (Doctors Without Borders) or Amnesty International. None of these can properly be viewed as 'global citizens,' nor do mere involvement in philanthropic activities provide a sufficient condition for it. Instead, they ought to be construed as *global statesmen* (a neutral term that could apply to any gender or organization). The ideal of global citizenship presupposes a much broader and more abstract concept that has no physical representation except as a collective consciousness and norm reflected in the actions of men. A *global statesman* is a person or an entity whose work seeks to address critical issues of the human condition and for which a universal acknowledgement would be desirable and justified.

Against this background, I sketch out two broad conceptual categories grounded in the competing notions of disintegration and reintegration. What will bring about the end of the state as we know it is immigration, legal and illegal. The *Economist* of September 12–18, 2015, carried the title *Exodus: Refugees, Compassion and Democracy*, and similarly *Time Magazine* in its Special Report of October 19, 2015, carried the title *Exodus: The Epic Migration to Europe and What Lies Ahead.* That these two internationally acclaimed publications would agree on essentially the same title for an epic event that began to unfold before the world in the last couple of years but saw its more dramatic surge in the summer of 2015 meant that such an event is of a memorable and historic proportion. "Rarely in modern history have so many been so desperate to flee; and now their brave and tragic journeys are reshaping Europe and the world" (Vick, 2015, pp. 38–39). The great migration of 2105 has seen waves and waves of Middle Easterners, Arabs, Asians and North Africans set out from Turkey or the coast of Libya riding in rubber boat contraptions across the Mediterranean onto the Greek Island of Lesbos or other places in Greece—*en route* to the rest of Europe.

It is the beginning of a long and arduous journey that no more respects national borders or the territorial integrity of European nations. As has been true since the creation of Israel on May 14, 1948, and the consequent crisis that has endured for decades, the Middle East and the Arab world continue to change the world in far-reaching ways. Now it seems to have outdone itself by what it has unleashed on Europe and the rest of the world. It is the beginning of the end of sovereign borders and a mirror by which the Westphalian state will see its imminent end. As thousands of immigrants, men and women and children crash through the borders of Europe with unrivaled brazenness, Europe has come face-to-face with the largest number of refugees ever experienced since WW II. The surge has seen countries like Bulgaria, Bosnia, Croatia, Hungary, Italy, Switzerland, France and even Germany losing control of their borders as their security personnel become overwhelmed or somewhat bewildered at the suddenness and ferocity of a new dynamic unfolding before their very eyes. As European policy makers dither and point fingers outwards but not inwards, as they dust off old and archaic lessons in the history of morals, unbeknownst to them, their lack of action or hesitance in stemming the tide and the confusing uncalculating messages from Germany has set in motion an unstoppable force that will change world history.

The *Time Magazine* of October 19, 2015 (pp. 40–41), indicates that from the beginning of the year to date, there were 630,000 illegal border crossings into Europe, and that Libya's migrant smuggling business generated $170 million in 2014 for sea crossing into Europe alone. It also states that 1 in 122 people worldwide is now a refugee or an internally displaced person or seeking asylum, such that if this population were a country, it would be the world's 24th largest. "More than 600,000 people have entered Europe so far in 2015, cascading in at a rate more than 10,000 a day—that forced underprepared, overwhelmed governments to quickly declared a crisis" (Vick, 2015, p. 40). While Germany alone received "200,000 asylum requests in 2014, its government has stated that it will welcome up to 800,000 refugees in 2015, and some estimates place the number as high as 1 million or more" (Bremmer, 2015, p. 85). "As new refugees keep pouring in, those granted asylum also have the right to bring their families later" (The *Economist*, October 10, 2015). Other European countries have pledged or are being 'rough-handled' into taking even more migrants and refugees. And yet "the Syrians—along with the Iraqis and Afghans—are only the most visible flotsam in a wider and scarcely less insistent stream of human beings, an almost tidal flow that has been running for decades from poorer (and oftentimes conflict-ridden) countries to richer" (Vick, 2015, p. 40). There is no end in sight, and the surge will continue for the foreseeable future.

The *Economist* of October 10, 2015 (p. 52), points to the rising German sentiment more succinctly, illustrating the public feeling that "the refugee crisis could change Germany even more than the reunification between East and West about 25 years ago." It states that back then, the task was to let that which belongs together grow together; but today's challenge is greater because what should now grow together has so far not belonged together. "Germans worry whether Muslim refugees will accept German norms of sexual equality, secularism, and German's special responsibility towards Israel and Jews" (The *Economist,* October 10, 2015, p. 52). But it may be too late, and if the past could be used as prologue, the tempered concern could better be reserved for history. For the more obvious reason, "Europe could never hope to copy America's history of a nation of immigrants; because outside the great cities, there is a lasting mold of geographically distinct nationalities that to the present day forms a potent reservoir of resistance to any project threatening it" (Kroes, 2000, p. 7). Although muted temporarily, that would also complicate future life in an increasingly multicultural Europe, and given "the incipient and protean character of the present situation, and the resistance of states to challenges to their authority" (Kivisto and Faist, 2007, p. 129); it is not too difficult to appreciate the fact that "any effort to expand the idea of citizenship to the global level has very little probability of success in the foreseeable future" (Kivisto and Faist, 2007, p. 128).

What can thus be learned from the great migrant and refugee wave of 2015 is that sovereign national borders are no more sacrosanct; they can be effectively breached very easily and at will. This very point is well documented along the US–Mexican border where any semblance of border control is only there mainly for the symbolism it represents. Second, to enter into a country, all that is needed is to have an excuse, organize as a group aided by media coverage, swarm the border of an adjoining or proximate state and crash through the gates to a new destination no matter how far it may be. The point is that if this same tactic is repeated two or more times and successfully executed in other regions of the world (like Oceania, Latin America or Asia) as has been done in Europe, that would then start on a global scale, the end of sovereign borders and territorial integrity as we know them. It is only then that an irrecoverable step toward the eventual demise of the sovereign state will begin.

As immigrants and refugees settle down in the various countries of Europe, history has shown that they are not likely to assimilate into the cultural practices and traditions of their host countries; instead, they cling together in their own separate territories or cultural enclaves where they continue to imbue among themselves and their children the cultural traditions, practices and religions of their home countries. Some immigrants may "bring with them their skills, their traditions, their politics, and their life of meaning; new members reconstruct the meaningful world of their host communities, hence their presence changes the nature of the shared and contested identity that allows a community or a nation to differentiate itself from others" (Fitzgerald, 1996, p. 229). As they increase in number, they seek increased political power as a means of bending the host culture or, in some cases, replacing it with their own, particularly as it concerns their own expressions of rights, freedom and religion. As they elect their own people into the governance and politics of their communities, they rely on their traditional and customary norms to create mini-cultural fiefdoms in the larger body politics of their host countries—while being protected and defended by the liberal justice system typical of most Western democracies.

Hybrid communities or cultural enclaves could evolve within a city block, a housing estate, a rural town or culturally distinct neighborhoods. As they expand outwards and attract more residents, they would begin to exercise a certain level of political or juridical power. Over time, they would become authorities in their own right and be in a position to contest for power and control against the existing government. Because the common denominator that binds all hybrid communities is a uniform culture, ethnicity, language or religion, any of these could become an organizing symbol. Incrementally, as the traditional authority of the state is weighed down from one crisis to another, hybrid communities may begin to seek even greater autonomy and jurisdiction within the specific boundaries of territory under their control. They will begin to exercise their autonomy in specific policy areas (even if on a de facto basis) until such a time that they are able to supplant or delegitimize the prevailing authority of the government. The cultural enclaves or the 'sanctuary cities' found in many of the big cities of the United States are good examples.

Because states would have become borderless territories, hybrid communities would represent the new configuration replacing the traditional state in all forms of social and political organization. Because there would be unique non-replicable cultural bonds for citizens within a hybrid community that distinguish it from the others, the consequent solidarity and political appeal would be insurmountable. As the new form of identity in a borderless world, as the traditional state disintegrates and dissolves under the weight of multiple tensions coalescing at the same time, hybrid communities would be able to consolidate their political and economic power across territorial jurisdictions. As they grow bigger and become more complex, the twin issues of sovereignty and autonomy would become the new basis for political and economic contestation. While it will take one concession and one victory at a time, but by the time all of these come to an end, hybrid communities would have taken over the role of the traditional state as the new "method of analyzing world geopolitical dynamics" (Eva, 1999, p. 33).

While some would opt for a straightforward declaration of sovereignty and independence, others would institute relational bonds of 'friendship' between them and similarly situated others with common cultural or economic interests. Nonetheless, it would be a world of 'To thy tents, O' Israel,' and to each according to his own fortunes and desires. This is how the modern state as we currently know it would inexorably and most likely sing its last *hurrah.* But "even if this sense of emergent political inadequacy did not in itself impair the normative appeal of the state form in question; it might readily expose the intrinsic limitations of that appeal in the face of the far harsher demands which are now placed on it" (Dunn, 1995, p. 5). While "unsettling changes in the boundaries of states around the world highlight certain weaknesses in territorial legitimation, it is equally useful to realize how fragile this legitimation is" (Hont, 1995, p. 173), particularly as European states struggle to take back control of their sovereign borders but are still not able to do so. How the conflict and crisis of a future world will unfold and their various manifestations can only be adjudged by the limit of human imagination; but what ought to be most evident is that the ideal of global citizenship, whether as status or as norm, would be severely contested.

Credits

This page provides information on some of the copyrighted material derived from the author's earlier works and extensively revised and update for some sections of the current work. All permissions to use such materials in whatever applicable form indicated have been duly granted.

Pages 2–5; 26–36 Excerpt from pp. 420–426 of "Of Citizenship, Virtue, and the Administrative Imperative: Deconstructing Aristotelian Civic Republicanism," by Kalu N. Kalu, as published in *Public Administration Review* 63(4): 418–427. Copyright © 2003 John Wiley & Sons Limited, UK.

Chapter 4 is an extensively revised version of an earlier work by the author that appeared under the same name in *Citizenship: A Reality Far From Ideal*, edited by Andrew Kakabadse, Nada Kakabadse, and Kalu N. Kalu, pp. 10–23. Copyright © 2009 Palgrave Macmillan, UK.

Pages 65–66, Excerpt from pp. 14–16 of *Citizenship: A Reality Far From Ideal*, edited by Andrew Kakabadse, Nada Kakabadse, and Kalu N. Kalu, pp. 10–23. Copyright © 2009 Palgrave Macmillan, UK.

Pages 75–76, Excerpt from pp. 11–13, 20 of *Citizenship: A Reality Far From Ideal*, edited by Andrew Kakabadse, Nada Kakabadse, and Kalu N. Kalu, pp. 10–23. Copyright © 2009 Palgrave Macmillan, UK.

Pages 76–78, Excerpt from pp. 126–127; 133–134 of "Institution-Building, not National-Building: A Structural-Functional Model," by Kalu N. Kalu, as published in *International Review of Administrative Sciences* 77(1): 119–137. Copyright © 2011 Sage Publications Limited, UK.

Chapter 7 is an updated version of an earlier work by the author that appeared under the same name in *Governance, Strategy and Policy*, edited by Nada Kakabadse and Andrew Kakabadse, pp. 73–93. Copyright © 2006 Palgrave Macmillan, UK.

Bibliography

Aberbach, J. D. and T. Christensen. 2003. Translating theoretical ideas into modern state reform: Economics-inspired reforms and competing models of governance. *Administration & Society,* 35(5): 491–509.

Adam, N. 2015. Migrants offer hope for German workforce. *The Wall Street Journal,* September 11, 2015.

Adonis, A. and G. Mulgan. 1994. Back to Greece: The scope for direct democracy. *Demos,* 3: 24–31.

Adorno, T. 1984. *Aesthetic theory*. London, England: RKP.

Agger, B. 1991. Critical theory, poststructuralism, postmodernism: Their sociological relevance. *Annual Review of Sociology,* 17: 105–131.

Alejandro, R. 1993. *Hermeneutics, citizenship, and the public sphere*. New York, NY: State University of New York Press.

Almond, G. A. and S. Verba. 1963. *The civic culture.* Boston, MA: Little, Brown & Co.

Anderson, B. 1983. *Imagined communities: Reflections on the origin and spread of nationalism*. New York, NY: Verso.

Aquino, K. and A. Reed. 2002. The self-importance of moral identity. *Journal of Personality and Social Psychology,* 83: 1423–1440.

Arendt, H. 1958. *The human condition.* Chicago, IL: The University of Chicago Press.

Aronowitz, S. 1989. Postmodernism and politics. *Social text, No. 21: Universal abandon? The politics of postmodernism*. Durham, NC: Duke University Press, 46–62.

Aristotle. 1948. *Politics*. Trans. by E. Barker. Oxford, UK: Clarendon Press.

Aristotle. 1962. *The Politics*. Trans. by T. A. Sinclair. New York, NY: Penguin Books.

Aristotle. 1985. *Nicomachean ethics.* Trans. by Terence Irwin. Indianapolis, IN: Hackett Publishing Company.

Armstrong, C. 2006. *Rethinking equality: The challenge of equal citizenship*. New York, NY: Manchester University Press.

Balsdon, J. P. V. D. 1979. *Romans and aliens*. Chapel Hill, NC: The University of North Carolina Press.

Beaudry, P. 2003. The economic policy that made the peace of Westphalia. Washington, DC: The Schiller Institute. http://www.schillerinstitute.org/strategic/treaty_of_westphalia.html. Accessed on September 23, 2015.

Beiner, R. 2003. *Liberalism, nationalism, citizenship: Essays on the problem of political community*. Vancouver, Canada: The University of British Columbia.

Bellamy, R. 2008. *Citizenship: A very short introduction.* New York, NY: Oxford University Press.

Bellamy, R. and D. Schecter. 1993. *Gramsci and the Italian state*. New York, NY: Manchester University Press.

Bendek, Z. M. 2002. Citizens of the future: Beyond normative conditions through the emergence of desirable collective properties. *Ethics,* 39: 189–195.

Bender, R. and W. Boston. 2015. Germany's welcome brings strains. *The Wall Street Journal*, December 5–6, p. A6.

Bertelli, A. M. and L. E. Lynn. 2003. Managerial responsibility. *Public Administration Review,* 63(3): 259–268.

Bhagwati, J. 1988. Global interdependence and international migration. In *Capital, technology, and labor in the new global economy* (Ed. by J. H. Cassing and S. L. Husted), 149–183. Washington, DC: American Enterprise Institute.

Bowman, J. S., J. P. West, E. M. Berman, and M. Van Wart. 2004. *The professional edge: Competencies in public service*. Armonk, NY: M. E. Sharpe.

Brams, J. S. 1997. Game theory and emotions. *Rationality and Society,* 9(1): 91–124.

Bravin, J. 2015. Ruling. *The Wall Street Journal*, Saturday/Sunday June 27–28, 2015, A6.

Bremmer, I. 2015. Europe divided: The migrant crisis tests the limits of E.U. cooperation. *Time Magazine,* 186(15–16): 84–85.

Brown, M. M. and J. Brudney. 2003. Learning organizations in the public sector? A study of police agencies employing information and technology to advance knowledge. *Public Administration Review,* 63(1): 30–43.

Bryce, J. 1993. *Hindrances to good citizenship*. New Brunswick, NJ: Transaction Publishers.

Burn, A. R. 1965. *The Pelican history of Greece*. Middlesex, England: Pelican Books.

Cabrera, L. 2010. *The practice of global citizenship*. Cambridge, UK: Cambridge University Press.

Cairns, A. 1993. The fragmentation of Canadian citizenship. In *Belonging: The meaning and future of Canadian citizenship*, ed., W. Kaplan, 181–220. Montreal, Canada: McGill-Queen's Press.

Calhoun, D. 1971. The human material. In *The case for participatory democracy*, ed. C.G. Benollo and D. Roussopoulis, 27–36. New York, NY: Grossman.

Carens, J. H. 2000. *Culture, citizenship, and community: A contextual exploration of justice and evenhandedness*. Oxford, England: Oxford University Press.

Carlton, E. 2006. *Politeia: Visions of the just society*. Madison, NJ: Fairleigh Dickinson University Press.

Carter, A. 1983. *Direct action*, 3rd ed. London, England: Housmans.

Carter, A. 2001. *The political theory of global citizenship*. New York, NY: Routledge.

Caspary, W. R. 2000. *Dewey on democracy*. Ithaca, NY: Cornell University Press.

Casson, L. 1998. *Everyday life in ancient Rome*. Baltimore, MD: The Johns Hopkins University Press.

Chandler, R. C. 1984. The public administrator as representative citizen: A new role for the new century. *Public Administration Review,* 44 (Special Issue): 196–206.

Charney, E. 2003. Identity and liberal nationalism. *American Political Science Review,* 97(2): 295–310.

Cicero. 1960. *Selected works* (Trans. by Michael Grant). Harmondsworth, Middlesex, England: Penguin Books Limited.

Cicero, M. T. 1913. *De Officiis* (With an English Translation by Walter Miller). Cambridge, MA: Harvard University Press.

Citrin, J., A. Lehman, M. Murakami, and K. Pearson. 2007. Testing Huntington: Is Hispanic immigration a threat to American identity? *Perspectives on Politics,* 5(1): 31–48.

Clair, J. A. 2015. Procedural injustice in the system of peer review and scientific misconduct. *Academy of Management Learning & Education,* 14(2): 159–172.

Cook, B. J. 1998. Politics, political leadership, and public management. *Public Administration Review,* 58(3): 225–231.

Cooper, T. 1984. Citizenship and professionalism in public administration. *Public Administration Review,* 44 (Special Issue): 143–149.

Crossley, N. 2001. Citizenship, intersubjectivity and the lifeworld. In *Culture and citizenship*, ed. N. Stevenson, 33–46. Thousand Oaks, CA: Sage Publications.

Crouch, C., K. Eder, and D. Tambini. 2001. *Citizenship, markets, and the state*. Oxford, England: Oxford University Press.

Croucher, S. L. 2004. *Globalization and belonging: The politics of identity in a changing world.* Lanham, MD: Rowman & Littlefield.

Dagger, R. 2002. Republican citizenship. In *Handbook of citizenship studies*, ed. E. F. Esin and B. S. Turner, 145–157. Thousand Oaks, CA: Sage Publications.

Dahl, R. A. 1982. *Dilemmas of pluralist democracy: Autonomy vs. control.* New Haven, CT: Yale University Press.

Damon, W. and D. Hart. 1992. Self-understanding and its role in social and moral development. In *Development psychology: An advanced textbook* (3rd ed), ed. M. H. Bornstein and E. Michael, 421–464. Hillsdale, NJ: Lawrence Erlbaum Associates Inc.

Davis, J. C. 1972. *The evangelic bureaucrat.* London, England: Tavistock.

De Tocqueville, A. 2000. *Democracy in America* (Trans. and Annot. by S. D. Grant). Indianapolis, IN: Hackett Publishing Company.

Denhardt, R. B. 1999. The future of public administration: Challenges to democracy, citizenship, and ethics. *Public Administration and Management: An Interactive Journal,* 1–10. http://pamij.com/99_4_2_Denhardt.html. Accessed on September 20, 2015.

Denhardt, R. 2011. *Theories of public organization.* Boston, MA: Wadsworth Cengage.

Downs, A. 1967. *An economic theory of democracy.* New York, NY: Free Press.

Derrida, J. 1978. *Writing and difference.* Chicago, IL: The University of Chicago Press.

Dowding, K. 2004. Are democratic and just institutions the same? In *Justice and democracy: Essays for Brian Barry*, ed. K. Dowding, R. E. Goodin, and C. Pateman, 25–39. New York, NY: Cambridge University Press.

Dreyfus, H. L. and P. Rabinow. 1983. *Michel Foucault: Beyond structuralism and hermeneutics*, 2nd ed. Chicago, IL: The University of Chicago Press.

Ducat, C. R. 2013. *Constitutional interpretation,* 10th ed. Boston, MA: Wadsworth Cengage.

Dunn, J. 1995. Introduction: Crisis of the nation state? In *Contemporary crisis of the nation state*?, ed. J. Dunn, 3–15. Oxford, UK: Blackwell.

Durant, R. 2006. Institutional values and the future administrative state. In *Revisiting Waldo's administrative state: Constancy and change in public administration,* ed. D. H. Rosenblum and H. E. McCurdy, 179–202. Washington, DC: Georgetown University Press.

Durkheim, E. 1994. Social facts. In *Readings in the philosophy of social science*, ed. M. Martin and L. C. McIntyre, 433–440. Cambridge, MA: MIT Press.

Dworkin, R. 1981. What is equality? Part 2: Equality of resources. *Philosophy and Public Affairs,* 10(4): 283–345.

Economist, The. 2015. Merkel at her limit. *The Economist*, 417(8959): 51–52, October 10.

Eley, G. and J. Palmowski. 2004. Citizenship and national identity in twentieth-century Germany. Proceedings of a conference organized by King's College London and the research project on "Constituting the German Nation: Constitutions and National Identity in Twentieth-Century Germany," King's College London, England, September 10–12, 2004.

Eva, F. 1999. International boundaries, geopolitics and the postmodern territorial discourse: The functional fiction. In *Boundaries, territory, and postmodernity*, ed. D. Newman, 32–52. London, England: Frank Cass.

Fagence, M. 1977. *Citizen participation in planning*. New York, NY: Pergamon Press.

Fitzgerald, K. 1996. *The face of the nation: Immigration, the state, and the national identity*. Stanford, CA: Stanford University Press.

Flathman, R. 1981. Citizenship and authority: A chastened view of citizenship. *News for Teachers of Political Science,* 30 (Summer): 9–19.

Foucault, M. 1988. *Politics, philosophy, culture*. New York, NY: Routledge.

Fox, C. J. 1996. Reinventing government as postmodern symbolic politics. *Public Administration Review,* 56(3): 256–262.

Fox, C. J. and H. T. Miller. 1995. *Postmodern public administration*. Thousand Oaks, CA: Sage.

Franck, T. M. 1999. *The empowered self: Law and society in the age of individualism*. New York, NY: Oxford University Press.

Frederickson, D. G. and H. G. Frederickson. 2007. *Measuring the performance of the hollow state.* Washington, DC: Georgetown University Press.

Frederickson, H. G. 1982. The recovery of civism in public administration. *Public Administration Review,* 42(6): 501–508.

Frederickson, H. G. 1991. Toward a theory of the public for public administration. *Administration & Society,* 22(4): 395–417.

Frederickson, H. G. 2000. Can bureaucracy be beautiful? *Public Administration Review,* 60(1): 47–53.

Frederickson, H. G. and R. C. Chandler. 1984. Citizenship and public administration. *Public Administration Review,* 44 (Special Issue): 97–209.

Fukuyama, F. 2006. Identity, immigration, and liberal democracy. *Journal of Democracy,* 17(2): 5–20.

Gabbard, S., R. Mines, and B. Boccalandro. 1994. *Migrant farmworkers: Pursuing security in unstable markets*. Washington, DC: ASP Research Report 5, U.S. Department of Labor.

Galston, W. 1991. *Liberal purposes: Goods, virtues, and duties in the liberal state*. Cambridge, UK: Cambridge University Press.

Gardner, W. L., and C. C. Cogliser, eds. 2009. Meso-modeling of leadership: Integrating micro-and macro-perspectives of leadership. *Leadership Quarterly,* 20(4): 493–650. Also see R. House, D. M. Rousseau, and M. Thomas-Hunt. 1995. The meso paradigm: A framework for integration of micro and macro organizational behavior. In *Research in organizational behavior* 17, ed. L. L. Cummings and B. M. Staw, 71–114. Greenwich, CT: JAI Press.

Gauthier, D. 1992. The liberal individual. In *Communitarianism and individualism*, ed. S. Avineri and A. de-Shalit, 151–164. New York, NY: Oxford University Press.

Gawthrop. L. C. 1998. The human side of public administration. The 1998 John Gauss lecture, 1–10. http://www.apsanet.org/PS/dec98/gawthrop.cfm. Accessed on September 20, 2015.

Gawthrop, L. C. and D. Waldo. 1984. Civis, civitas, and civilitas: A new focus for the year 2000. *Public Administration Review,* 44 (Special Issue): 101–111.

George, A. 2005. Domestic constraints on regime change in U.S. foreign policy: The need for policy legitimacy. In *American foreign policy: Theoretical essays*, ed. G. J. Ikenberry, 333–357. New York, NY: Pearson Longman.

Gerschenkron, A. 1962. *Economic backwardness in historical perspective: A book of essays*. Cambridge, MA: Harvard University Press.

Gifford, C. 2004. National and post-national dimensions of citizenship education in the U.K. *Citizenship Studies,* 8(2): 145–158.

Gilbert, R. 1992. Citizenship, education and postmodernity. *British Journal of Sociology of Education,* 13(1): 51–68.

Glenn, E. 2000. Citizens and inequality: Historical and global perspectives. *Social Problems,* 47(1): 1–20.

Goldin, I. and K. Reinert. 2006. *Globalization for development: Trade, finance, aid, migration, and policy.* Washington, DC: The World Bank/Palgrave Macmillan.

Goodin, R. E. 2004. Democracy, justice, impartiality. In *Justice and democracy: Essays for Brian Barry*, ed. K. Dowding, R. E. Goodin, and C. Pateman, 97–111. New York, NY: Cambridge University Press.

Goodsell, C. T. 2015. *The new case for bureaucracy*. Thousand Oaks, CA: Sage.

Gorham, E. 1995. Social citizenship and its fetters. *Polity,* 28(1): 25–47.

Gorman, R. F. 1992. Citizenship, obligation, and exile in the Greek and Roman experience. *Public Affairs Quarterly,* 6(1): 5–22.

Gould, C. C. 2001. Two concepts of universality and the problem of cultural relativism. In *Cultural identity and the nation-state*, ed. C. C. Gould and P. Pasquino, 67–84. Lanham, MD: Rowman & Littlefield Publishers.

Gross, F. 1999. *Citizenship and ethnicity: The growth and development of a democratic multiethnic institution.* Westport, CT: Greenwood Press.

Gutmann, A. 1992. Communitarian critics of liberalism. In *Communitarianism and individualism*, ed. S. Avineri and A. de-Shalit, 120–136. New York, NY: Oxford University Press.

Habermas, J. 1979. *Communication and the evolution of society*. Boston, MA: Beacon.

Habermas, J.1984. *The theory of communicative action, Vol. 1*. Boston, MA: Beacon.

Halliday, F. 2000. Global governance: Prospects and problems. *Citizenship Studies,* 4(1): 19–34.

Halisi, C. R. D., P. J. Kaiser, and S. N. Ndegwa. 1998. The multiple meanings of citizenship—Rights, identity, and social justice in Africa. *Africa Today,* 45: 337–350, p. 340.

Halvorsen, K. 2003. Assessing the effects of public participation. *Public Administration Review,* 63(5): 535–543.

Hansen, P. 1993. *Hannah Arendt: Politics, history and citizenship*. Stanford, CA: Stanford University Press.

Hart, D. K. 1984. The virtuous citizen, the honorable bureaucrat as public administrator. *Public Administration Review,* 44 (Special Issue): 111–120.

Haste, H. 2004. Constructing the citizen. *Political Psychology,* 25(3): 413–439.

Hearnshaw, F. J. C., ed. 1981. *Medieval contributions to modern civilization*. London, England: George G. Harrap & Co. Limited.

Heater, D. 1990. *Citizenship: The civic ideal in world history, politics and education*. London, England: Longman.

Heater, D. 1999. *What is citizenship*? Cambridge, UK: Polity Press.

Held, D.1989. *Political theory and the modern state: Essays on state, power, and democracy*. Stanford, CA: Stanford University Press.

Held, D. 2005. Globalization, corporate practice, and cosmopolitan social standards. In *Global responsibilities: Who must deliver on human rights?*, ed. A. Kuper, 185–204. New York, NY: Routledge.

Hobbes, T. 1994. *Leviathan* (ed. E. Curly based on the Latin edition of 1668). Indianapolis, IN: Hackett Publishing Company, Inc.

Hogan, D. 1997. The logic of protection: Citizenship, justice and political community. In *Citizenship education and the modern state*, ed. K. J. Kennedy, 27–53. London, England: The Farmer Press.

Holzer, M. 1999. Communicating commitment: Public administration as a calling. *Public Administration: An Interactive Journal*. http://pamij.com/99_4_2_Holzer.html. Accessed on September 20, 2015.

Home Office. 1985. *Review of public order law*. London, England: HMSO.

Hont, I. 1995. The permanent crisis of a divided mankind: 'Contemporary crisis of the nation state' in historical perspective. In *Contemporary crisis of the nation state*? ed. J. Dunn, 166–231. Oxford, UK: Blackwell.

Horkheimer, M. 1972. *Critical theory*. New York, NY: Herder & Herder.

Hunt, J. G. 1996. *Leadership: A new synthesis*. Newbury Park, CA: Sage.

Huntington, S. P. 1996. *The clash of civilizations and the remaking of world order*. New York, NY: Simon & Schuster, 272–291.

Irvin, R. A. and J. Stansbury. 2004. Citizen participation in decision making: Is it worth the effort? *Public Administration Review,* 64(1): 55–65.

Isin, E. F. and P. K. Wood. 1999. *Citizenship and identity*. Thousand Oaks, CA: Sage. Publications.

Jacobson, D. 1998. State and society in a world unbound. In *Public rights, public rules: Constituting citizens in the world polity and national policy*, ed. C. L. McNeely, 41–57. New York, NY: Garland Publishing Inc.

Jacobsen, D. 1996. *Rights across borders: Immigration and the decline of citizenship.* Baltimore, MD: The Johns Hopkins University Press. Also see 1990. Constructing the state extra-territorially: Jurisdictional discourse, the national interest and transnational norms. *Harvard Law Review,* 103(6): 1273–1305, p. 1297.

Janoski, T. and B. Gran. 2002. Political citizenship: Foundations of rights. In *Handbook of citizenship studies*, ed. E. F. Isin, and B. S. Turner, 13–52. London, England: Sage Publications.

Jaspers, K. 1932. *Philosophische Weltorientierung I.* Berlin: Springer.

Jennings, M. K. 1997. Political participation in the Chinese countryside. *American Political Science Review,* 91(2): 361–372.

Jepperson, R. L. 1991. Institutions, institutional effects, and institutionalization. In *The New Institutionalism in Organizational Analysis*, ed. W. W. Powell and P. J. DiMaggio, 143–163. Chicago, IL: University of Chicago Press.

Johnson, C. 2004. *The sorrows of empire: Militarism, secrecy, and the end of the republic.* New York, NY: Henry Holt & Company.

Joyce, P. 2002. *The politics of protest: Extra-parliamentary politics in Britain since 1970.* Basingstoke, UK: Palgrave Macmillan.

Kakabadse, A., N. K. Kakabadse., and A. Kouzmin. 2003. Reinventing the democratic governance project through information technology? A growing agenda for debate. *Public Administration Review,* 63(1): 44–60.

Kalu, K. N. 2003a. Of citizenship, virtue, and the administrative imperative: Deconstructing Aristotelian civic republicanism. *Public Administration Review,* 63(4): 422–423, p. 421.

Kalu, K. N. 2003b. Entrepreneurs or conservators? Contractarian principles of bureaucratic performance. *Administration & Society,* 35(5): 539–563.

Kalu, K. N. 2007. Global governance and national governance: How mutually exclusive? In *Handbook of globalization, governance, and public administration*, ed. A. Farazmand and J. Pinkowski, 297–312. Boca Raton, FL: CRC Press/Taylor & Francis Group.

Kalu, K. N. 2008a. Managing people and information in complex organizations. In *Handbook of research on public information technology*, ed. G. D. Garson and M. Khosrow-Pour, 638–649. Hershey, PA: Idea Group, Inc. www.idea-group-ref.com.

Kalu, K. N. 2008b. Securing homeland security: Immigrant responses to state and citizenship. In *Homeland security handbook*, ed. J. Pinkowski, 59–75. Boca Raton, FL: CRC Press.

Kalu, K. N. 2009. *State power, autarchy, and political conquest in Nigerian federalism*. Lanham, MD: Rowman & Littlefield Publishers.

Kalu, K. N. 2011. Institution-building, not nation-building: A structural-functional model. *International Review of Administrative Sciences,* 77(1): 119–137.

Kay, S. 2015. *Global security in the twenty-first century: The quest for power and the search for peace*. Lanham, MD: Rowman & Littlefield Publishers.

Keller, A. G. 1902. *Homeric society: A sociological study of the Iliad and Odyssey*. London, England: Longmans, Green & Co.

Kierkegaard, S. 1946. The present age: A literary review. In *Kierkegaard anthology*, ed. R. Bretall, 258–269. Princeton, NJ: Princeton University Press.

King, D. S. and J. Waldron. 1988. Citizenship, social citizenship and the defense of welfare provision. *British Journal of Political Science,* 18(4): 415–443.

Kirlin, J. J. and M. K. Kirlin. 2002. Strengthening effective government-citizen connections through greater civic engagement. *Public Administration Review,* 62 (Special Issue): 80–84.

Kivisto, P. and T. Faist. 2007. *Citizenship: Discourse, theory, and transnational prospects*. Malden, MA: Blackwell Publishing.

Klijn, E.-H. 2002. Governing networks in the hollow state: Contracting out, process management or combination of the two? *Public Management Review,* 4(2): 149–165.

Kolb, D. 1990. *Postmodern sophistications: Philosophy, architecture, and tradition*. Chicago, IL: The University of Chicago Press.

Kroes, R. 2000. *Them and us: Questions of citizenship in a globalizing world*. Urbana, IL: University of Illinois Press.

Kuhnert, K. W. 1994. Transformational leadership: Developing people through delegation. In *Improving organizational effectiveness through transformational leadership*, ed. B. M. Bass and B. J. Avolio, 10–25. Thousand Oaks, CA: Sage Publications.

Kukathas, C. 1995. Are there any cultural rights? In *The rights of minority cultures*, ed. W. Kymlicka, 228–256. New York, NY: Oxford University Press.

Kymlicka, W. 1995. *Multicultural citizenship: A liberal theory of minority rights*. New York, NY: Oxford University Press.

Kymlicka, W. 1998. Multicultural citizenship. In *The citizenship debates: A reader*, ed. G. Shafir, 167–188. Minneapolis, MN: University of Minnesota Press.

Kymlicka, W. and W. Norman. 1994. Return of the citizen: A survey of recent work on citizenship theory. *Ethics,* 104(2): 352–80.

Lacey, W. K. 1968. *The family in classical Greece*. Ithaca, NY: Cornell University Press.

Lagos, T. G. 2013. Parallel polis and the Arab Spring: The Internet as layer, difference, and engine of democratic renewal. In *Culture and civilization: Cosmopolitanism and the global polity, Vol. 5*, ed. G. R. Ricci, 161–180. New Brunswick, NJ: Transaction Publishers.

Laski, H. J. 1935. *The state in theory and practice*. New York, NY: The Viking Press.

Light, P. 1999. *The new public service*. Washington, DC: Brookings Institution.

Linklater, A. 2007. *Critical theory and world politics: Citizenship, sovereignty and humanity*. New York, NY: Routledge.

Locke, J. 1963. *The two treatises of government*, ed. P. Laslett. New York, NY: Mentor.

London, S. 1994. *Electronic democracy: A literature survey*. Paper prepared for the Kettering Foundation, Santa Barbara, CA.

Long, N. E. 1981. Cities without citizens. In *Cities without citizens*, ed. B. R. Schuster, 4–21. Philadelphia, PA: Center for the Study of Federalism, Temple University.

Lowi, T. J. 1981. The two cities of Norton Long. In *Cities without citizens*, ed. B. R. Schuster, 30–36. Philadelphia, PA: Center for the Study of Federalism Temple University.

Lyotard, J.-F. 1984. *The postmodern condition: A report on knowledge*. Manchester, UK: Manchester University Press.

MacIntyre, A. 1988. *Whose justice? Which rationality*? Notre Dame, IN: University of Notre Dame Press.

MacIntyre, A.1992. Justice as virtue: Changing conceptions. In *Communitarianism and individualism*, ed. S. Avineri and A. de-Shalit, 51–64. New York, NY: Oxford University Press.

March, J. G. and J. P. Olsen. 1989. *Rediscovering institutions: The organizational basis of politics*. New York, NY: The Free Press.

Marcuse, H. 1978. *The aesthetic dimension*. Boston, MA: Beacon Press.

Marshall, T. H. 1965. *Class, citizenship, and social development*. New York, NY: Doubleday.

Marshall, T. H. 1950. *Citizenship and social class and other essays*. Cambridge, England: Cambridge University Press. Also see K. Rubenstein. 2000. Citizenship and the centenary: Inclusion and exclusion in 20th century Australia. *Melbourne University Law Review*, 24: 576–608.

Martin, M. 1994. Taylor on interpretation and the sciences of man. In *Readings in the philosophy of social science*, ed. M. Martin and L. C. McIntyre, 259–279. Cambridge, MA: MIT Press.

Mascolo, G. 2006. America's illegals: A nation of immigrants clashes over the future. *Spiegel Magazine Online* (International), pp. 1–9. http://service.spiegel.de/cache/international/spiegel/0,1518,409683,00.html. Accessed on April 6, 2006.

Matheson, P. E. 1897. Citizenship. *International Journal of Ethics*, 8(1): 22–40.

May, J. V. 1971. *Citizen participation: A review of the literature*. Davis, CA: University of California Press.

McCarthy, T. 1996. *The critical theory of Habermas*. Cambridge, MA: MIT Press.

McGregor, E. B. 1984. Citizenship and the professional public servant. *Public Administration Review*, 44 (Special Issue): 126–132.

Mead, G. H. 1967. *Mind, self, and society from the standpoint of a social behaviorist* (Ed. with an introduction by Charles W. Morris). Chicago, IL: University of Chicago Press.

Mearsheimer, J. J. 2001. *The tragedy of great power politics*. New York, NY: W. W. Norton & Company.

Messia, H., L. Borghese, and J. Hanna. 2015. Muslim migrants threw Christians overboard. CNN, p. 1. http://www.cnn.com/2015/04/16/europe/italy-migrants-christians-thrown-overboard. Accessed on September 5, 2015.

Migdal, J. S. 2001. *State in society: Studying how states and societies transform and constitute one another*. New York, NY: Cambridge University Press.

Mill, J. S. 2007. Utilitarianism. In *Justice: A reader*, ed. M. J. Sandel, 14–47. New York, NY: Oxford University Press.

Miller, D. 1992. Community and citizenship. In *Communitarianism and individualism*, ed. S. Avineri and A. de-Shalit, 85–100. New York, NY: Oxford University Press.

Milward, H. B. and K. G. Provan. 2000. Governing the hollow state. *Journal of Public Administration Research and Theory*, 10(2): 359–379.

Milward, H. B., K. G. Provan., and B. A. Else. 1993. What does the hollow state look like? In *Public management: The state of the art*, ed. B. Bozeman, 309–322. San Francisco, CA: Jossey Bass.

Mo, J. 1995. Domestic institutions and international bargaining: The role of Agent Veto in two-level games. *American Political Science Review*, 89: 914–924.

Morgan, E. S. 1998. *Inventing the people: The rise of popular sovereignty in England and America*. New York, NY: W. W. Norton.

Mosher, W. E., ed. 1941. *Introduction to responsible citizenship*. New York, NY: Holt and Co.

Murphy, M. and S. Harty. 2003. Post-sovereign citizenship. *Citizenship Studies,* 7(2): 181–197.

North, D. 1990. *Institutions, institutional change, and economic performance*. Cambridge, UK: Cambridge University Press.

North, D. and B. Weingast. 1989. Constitutions and commitment: The evolution of institutions governing public choice in seventeenth-century England. *Journal of Economic History,* 49(4): 813–832.

Northouse, P. G. 2010. *Leadership: Theory and practice*, 5th ed. Thousand Oaks, CA: Sage.

Nozick, R. 1974. *Anarchy, state and utopia*. New York, NY: Basic Books.

Nussbaum, M. 1990. Aristotelian social democracy. In *Liberalism and the good,* ed. R. B. Douglass, G. M. Mara, and H. S. Richardson, 203–252. New York, NY: Routledge.

Nussbaum, M. and A. Sen. 1989. Internal criticism and Indian rationalist traditions. In *Relativism: Interpretation and confrontation*, ed. M. Krauz, 299–325. Notre Dame, IN: University of Notre Dame Press.

Oldfield, A. 1990. Citizenship: An unnatural practice. *Political Quarterly,* 61(2): 177–87.

Oldfield, A. 1998. Citizenship and community: Civic republicanism and the modern world. In *The citizenship debates: A reader*, ed. G. Shafir, 75–89. Minneapolis, MN: University of Minnesota Press.

Oliver, J. E. 2000. City size and civic involvement in metropolitan America. *American Political Science Review,* 94(2): 361–381.

Olson, R. 1996. Information technology in home health care. In *Future care: Responding to the demand for change*, ed. C. Bezold and E. Mayer, 87–103. New York, NY: Faulkner.

Orr, M., and D. M. West. 2007. Citizen evaluations of local police: Personal experience or symbolic attitudes? *Administration & Society,* 38(6): 649–668.

Osborne, D. and T. Gaebler. 1992. *Reinventing government: How the entrepreneurial spirit is transforming the public sector*. New York, NY: Penguin Books.

Oslo, R. 1996. Information technology in home health care. In *Future care: Responding to the demand for change*, ed. C. Bezold and E. Mayer, 87–103. New York, NY: Faulkner.

O'Toole, L. J. 1990. Legitimacy, legitimation, and public administration: Rejoinder to Stever. *Administration and Society,* 22(1): 58–65.

Palmer, R. E. 1977. Postmodernity and hermeneutics. *Boundary 2*, 5(2): 363–394, Winter.

Parekh, B. 2008. *A new politics of identity: Political principles for an international world.* New York, NY: Palgrave Macmillan.

Parsons, T. 1977. *Social systems and the evolution of action theory*. New York, NY: The Free Press.

Pawar, B. S., and K. K. Eastman. 1997. The nature and implications of contextual influences on transformational leadership: A conceptual examination. *Academy of Management Review,* 22(1): 95.

Perry, J. and M. C. Katula. 2001. Does service affect citizenship? *Administration & Society,* 33(3): 20–72.

Phenomenology Online. 2015. http://www.phenomenologyonline.com/inquiry/methods-procedures/reflective-methods. Accessed September 20.

Plato. 1871. *The great dialogues of Plato,* Vol. II (Trans. by B. Jowett). New York, NY: Charles Scribner & Co.

Plato. 1955. *The Republic*. New York, NY: Penguin Books.

Pocock, J. G. A. 1975. *The Machiavellian moment: Florentine political thought and the Atlantic republican tradition*. Princeton, NJ: Princeton University Press.

Poole, R. 1999. *Nation and identity*. London, England: Routledge.

Procacci, G. 2001. Poor citizens: Social citizenship versus individualization of welfare. In *Citizenship, markets, and the state*, ed. C. Crouch, K. Eder, and D. Tambini, 49–68. New York, NY: Oxford University Press.

Przeworski, A. and J. Vreeland. 2002. A statistical model of bilateral cooperation. *Political Analysis,* 10.

Putnam, R. D. 1988. Diplomacy and domestic politics: The logic of two-level games. *International Organizations,* 42: 427–460.

Putnam, R. D. 1993. *Making democracy work: Civic traditions in modern Italy*. Princeton, NJ: Princeton University Press.

Putnam, R. D. 1995a. Bowling alone: America's declining social capital. *Journal of Democracy,* 6(1): 65–78.

Putnam, R. D. 1995b. Turning in, turning out: The strange disappearance of social capital in America. *Political Science & Politics,* 28: 664–683.

Putnam, R. D. 2002. Bowling together: The United States of America. *The American Prospect,* 13(3): 20–22.

Quackenbush, S. L. 2015. *International conflict: Logic and evidence*. Thousand Oaks, CA: Sage-CQ.

Rabinow, P., ed. 1991. *The Foucault reader: An introduction to Foucault's thought.* London, England: Penguin Publishers.

Racine, D. P. 1995. The welfare state, citizens, and immersed civil servants. *Administration and Society,* 26(4): 434–463.

Raskin, M. G. 2004. *Liberalism: The genius of American ideals*. Lanham, MD: Rowman & Littlefield Publishers, Inc.

Rawls, J. 1971. *A theory of justice*. Cambridge, MA: Harvard University Press.

Rawls, J. 2007. Justice as fairness. In *Justice: A reader*, ed. M. J. Sandel, 203–221. New York, NY: Oxford University Press.

Reeve, C. D. C. and P. L. Miller, ed. 2006. *Introductory readings in ancient Greek and Roman philosophy*. Indianapolis, IN: Hackett Publishing Company, Inc.

Rein, M.1969. Social planning: The search for legitimacy. *Journal of American Institute of Planners,* 35: 233–244.

Roberts, N. 2004. Public deliberation in an age of direct citizen participation. *American Review of Public Administration,* 34(4): 315–353.

Roche, M. 2002. Social citizenship: Grounds for social change. In *Handbook of citizenship studies*, ed. E. F. Esin and B. S. Turner, 69–86. Thousand Oaks, CA: Sage Publications.

Rorty, R. 1989. *Contingency, irony, and solidarity*. Cambridge, England: Cambridge University Press). http://www.equip.org/article/the-postmodern-challenge. Accessed on September 20, 2015.

Rosenbaum, N. N. 1978. Citizen participation and democratic theory. In *Participation in America*, ed. S. Langton, 43–54. Toronto, Canada: D. C. Heath & Co.

Rubenstein, K. 2000. Citizenship and the centenary: Inclusion and exclusion in 20th century Australia. *Melbourne University Law Review,* 24: 576–608.

Salvi, S. 2015. The original list of sanctuary cities, USA. http://ojjpac.org/sanctuary.asp. Accessed on October 13, 2015.

Sandel, M. J. 1982. *Liberalism and the limits of justice*. New York, NY: Cambridge University Press.

Sandel, M. J. 1998. *Liberalism and the limits of justice*, 2nd ed. New York, NY: Cambridge University Press.

Sandel, M. J., ed. 2007. *Justice: A reader*. New York, NY: Oxford University Press.

Sandel, M. J. 2009. Justice: *What's the right thing to do*? New York, NY: Farrah, Straus and Giroux.

Sartre, J.-P. (Ed. and intro. by R. D. Cumming). 1965. *The philosophy of J.-P. Sartre*. New York, NY: Vintage Books.

Saunders, J. T. 1966. ed. *Greek and Roman philosophy after Aristotle*. New York, NY: The Free Press.

Schattle, H. 2008. *The practices of global citizenship*. Lanham, MD: Rowman & Littlefield Publishers.

Schneider, D. 2000. Symbolic citizenship, nationalism and the distant state: The United States Congress in the 1996 debate on immigration reform. *Citizenship Studies,* 4(3): 255–273.

Schulte-Sasse, J. 1986. Modernity and modernism, postmodernity and postmodernism: Framing the issue. *Cultural Critique*, 5: 5–22.

Scott, W. R. 2014. *Institutions and organizations: Ideas, interests, and identities*, 4th ed. Thousand Oaks, CA: Sage.

Seaver, R. C. 1968. The dilemma of citizen participation. In *Citizen participation in urban development* (Vol. I), ed. H. B. C. Spiegel, 61–71. Washington, DC: NTL Institute for Applied Behavioral Science.

Sementelli, A. 2009. Citizenship and the individual. In *Citizenship: A reality far from ideal*, ed. A. Kakabadse, N. Kakabadse, and K. N. Kalu, 49–62. Basingstoke, UK: Palgrave Macmillan.

Shain, Y. 1999. *Marketing the American creed abroad: Diasporas in the U.S. and their homelands*. New York, NY: Cambridge University Press.

Shepsle, K. A. 1989. Studying institutions: Lessons from the rational choice approach. *Journal of Theoretical Politics,* 1: 131–147.

Shepsle, K. A. and B. Weingast. 1995. *Positive theories of congressional institutions*. Ann Arbor, MI: The University of Michigan Press.

Sigel, R. S. and M. B. Hoskin. 1981. *The political involvement of adolescents*. New Brunswick, NJ: Rutgers University Press.

Simonsen, W. and M. D. Robbins. 2000. *Citizen participation in resource allocation*. Boulder, CO: Westview Press.

Smith, A. 1999. Testing theories of strategic choice. *American Journal of Political Science,* 43: 1254–1283.

Smith, R. M. 1997. *Civic ideals: Conflicting visions of citizenship in U.S. history*. New Haven, CT: Yale University Press.

Smith, R. M. 2005. The challenges facing American citizenship today. *PS: Political Science & Politics,* 38: 679–681.

Sniderman, P. 1981. *A question of loyalty.* Berkeley, CA: University of California Press.

Somjee, A. H. 1968. *The political theory of John Dewey*. New York, NY: Teachers College Press, Columbia University.

Soutphommasane, T. 2012. *The virtuous citizen: Patriotism in a multicultural society*. New York, NY: Cambridge University Press.

Spiegel, H. B. C. and S. D. Mittenthal. 1968. The many faces of citizen participation: A bibliographic overview. In *Citizen participation in urban development*, ed. H. B. C. Spiegel, 3–17. Washington, DC: NTL Institute for Applied Behavioral Science.

Stalker, P. 2001. *The no-nonsense guide to international migration*. Oxford, England: New Internationalist Publication.

Stephens, B. 2015. Farewell to the era of no fences, *The Wall Street Journal*, Tuesday September 8, A11.

Stephens, O. H. Jr., J. M. Scheb II, and C. Glennon. 2015. *American Constitutional Law Volume II: Civil rights and liberties*, 6th ed. Stamford, CT: Cengage Learning.

Stevenson, N. 1997. Globalization, national cultures and cultural citizenship. *The Sociological Quarterly,* 38(1): 41–66.

Stever, J. A. 1993. Technology, organization, freedom: The organizational theory of John Dewey. *Administration and Society,* 24(4): 419–443.

Taylor, C. 1992. Atomism. In *Communitarianism and individualism*, ed. S. Avineri and A. de-Shalit, 29–50. New York, NY: Oxford University Press.

Terry, L. D. 1990. Leadership in the administrative state: The concept of administrative conservatorship. *Administration and Society,* 21(4): 395–412.

Terry, L. D. 2005. The thinning of administrative institutions in the hollow state. *Administration & Society,* 37(4): 426–444.

Thornburgh, N. 2006. Shadow workers. *Time*, 167(6): 34–45, February 6.

Tidrick, K. 2006. *Gandhi: A political and spiritual life*. London, England: I. B. Tauris.

Tilly, C., ed. 1996. *Citizenship, identity and social history: International review of social history, supplement 3*. Cambridge, England: Cambridge University Press.

Tilly, C. 2008. *Explaining social processes*. Boulder, CO: Paradigm Publishers.

Tololyan, K. 1991. Uprooted peoples enter a new age of migration. *Newsday*, September 8, p. 36.

Tosi, H. L. 2009. *Theories of organization.* Thousand Oaks, CA: Sage Publications.

Trice, H. M. and J. M. Beyer. 1993. *The cultures of work organizations*. Upper Saddle River, NJ: Prentice Hall, Inc.

Tsebelis, G. 1995. Decision making in political systems. *British Journal of Political Science,* 25: 289–326.

Tsebelis, G. 2002. *Veto players: How political institutions work.* Princeton, NJ: Princeton University Press.

Tully, J. 1995. *Strange multiplicity: Constitutionalism in an age of diversity*. Cambridge, England: Cambridge University Press.

Turner, B. S. 1986. *Citizenship and capitalism: The debate over reformism*. London, England: Allen and Unwin.

Turner, B. S. 1990. Outline of a theory of citizenship. *Sociology,* 24(2): 189–217.

van Gunsteren, H. 1998. *A theory of citizenship: Organizing plurality in contemporary democracies*. Boulder, CO: Westview Press.

Vaubel, R. 1986. A public choice approach to international organization. *Public Choice,* 51: 39–57.

Ventriss, C. 2007. A substantive view of ethical citizenship in public affairs. *Public Performance & Management Review,* 31(1): 38–58.

Verba, S. 1996. The citizen as respondent: Sample surveys and American democracy. *American Political Science Review,* 90(1):1–7.

Verba, S., K. Lehman Schlozman, and H. E. Brady.1995. *Voice and equality: Civic volunteerism in American democracy*. Cambridge, MA: Harvard University Press.

Verba, S., K. Lehman Schlozman, H. E. Brady, and N. Nie. 1990. *American citizen participation study, 1990*, ICPSR Version 6635. Chicago, IL: University of Chicago, National Opinion Research Center (Producer), 1995; Ann Arbor, MI: Inter-university Consortium for Political and Social Research (Distributor), 1995.

Verba, S. and N. Nie. 1972. *Participation in America: Political democracy and social equality*. New York, NY: Harper & Row.

Vick, K. 2015. The great migration. *Time Magazine,* 186(15–16): 38–49.

Vigoda, E. 2002. From responsiveness to collaboration: Governance, citizens, and the next generation of public administrators. *Public Administration Review,* 62(5): 527–540.

Voegelin, E. 1957. *Plato*. Columbia, MO: University of Missouri Press.

Walker R. B. J. 1999. Citizen after the modern subject. In *Cosmopolitan citizenship*, ed. K. Hutchings and R. Dannreuther, 171–200.

Walzer, M. 1970. *Obligation: Essays on disobedience, war and citizenship*. Cambridge, MA: Harvard University Press.

Walzer, M. 1983. *Spheres of justice: A defense of pluralism and equality*. New York, NY: Basic Books.

Walzer, M. 1989. Citizenship. In *Political innovation and conceptual change*, ed. T. Ball, J. Farr, and R. L. Hanson, 211–219. Cambridge, UK: Cambridge University Press.

Walzer, M. 1995. Pluralism: A political perspective. In *The rights of minority cultures*, ed. W. Kymlicka, 139–154. New York, NY: Oxford University Press.

Washington Post, The. 1998. New law in Mexico, May 31.

Washington Post, The. 2015. Frustrated migrants blame U.S. for their predicament. http://a.msn.com/01/en-us/AAeboFI?ocid=se. Accessed on September 12, 2015, p. 1.

Weber, Max. 1947. *The theory of social and economic organization* (Trans. by T. Parsons). New York, NY: Free Press.

Weber, Max. 1998. Citizenship in ancient and Medieval cities. In *The citizenship debates: A reader*, ed. G. Shafir, 43–49. Minneapolis, MN: University of Minnesota Press.

Weeks, E. C. 2000. The practice of deliberative democracy: Results from four large-scale trials. *Public Administration Review*, 60(4): 360–372.

Werner, P. 1977. *Life in Greece in ancient times*. Barcelona, Spain: Liber S. A.

Wexler, P. 1990. Citizenship in the semiotic society. In *Theories of modernity and postmodernity*, ed. B. Turner, 164–175. London, England: Sage.

White, S. 2000. Social rights and the social contract: Political theory and the new welfare politics. *British Journal of Political Science*, 30(3): 507–532.

Wilson, W. 1887. The study of administration. *Political Science Quarterly*, 2(2): 197–222.

Young, I. M. 1989. Polity and group difference: A critique of the ideal of universal citizenship. *Ethics*, 99(2): 250–274.

Young, I. M. 1998. Polity and group difference: A critique of the ideal of universal citizenship. In *The citizenship debates: A reader*, ed. G. Shafir, 263–290. Minneapolis, MN: University of Minnesota Press.

Yukl, G. 2010. *Leadership in organizations*. Upper Saddle River, NJ: Prentice Hall Inc.

Digital Sources

http://history1900s.about.com/od/people/a/gandhi.htm?p=1. Accessed on August 15, 2015.

http://www.indianchild.com/mahatma_gandhi.htm. Accessed on August 15, 2015.

Index